The
ROYAL PALACE OF PHNOM PENH
and Cambodian Royal Life

The
ROYAL PALACE OF PHNOM PENH
and Cambodian Royal Life

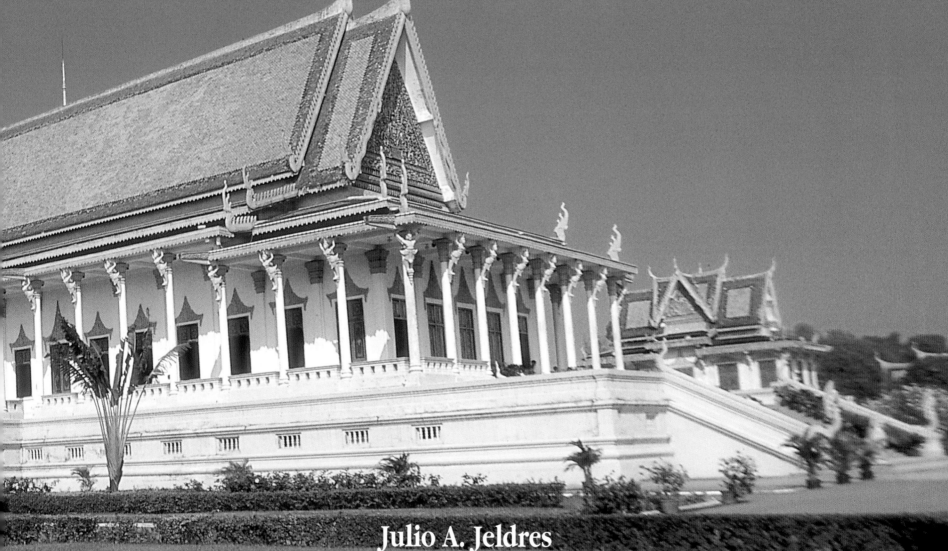

Julio A. Jeldres
Somkid Chaijitvanit

The Royal Palace of Phnom Penh and Cambodian Royal Life
Published by Post Books, The Post Publishing Plc.
136 Na Ranong Road, off Sunthorn Kosa Road,
Klong Toey, Bangkok 10110, Thailand
Tel: (662) 240-3700 ext. 1691-2
Fax: (662) 671-9698
e-mail: postbooks@bangkokpost.co.th
http://www.bangkokpost.net/postbooks/

Texts and photographs © Julio A. Jeldres 1999

First published in 1999
Printed by Allied Printers, The Post Publishing Plc.

National Library of Thailand Cataloging-in-Publication Data
Jeldres, Julio A.
The Royal Palace of Phnom Penh and Cambodian Royal Life.--
Bangkok : Post Books, 1999. 132 p.
1. Cambodia--History. 2. Palace--Cambodia
I. Somkid Chaijitvanit, photos. II. Title. 959.6

ISBN: 974-202-047-7

Photographs: Somkid Chaijitvanit (except where indicated otherwise.)
Computer illustrations: Sataporn Kawewong
Design and layout: Watchara Ritmahan
Set in: AGaramond, Aplgaram, Helvetica,
PSL-Chamnarn and PSL-ThaiCommon

The author respectfully dedicates this book to
His Majesty Preah Bat Samdech Preah
Norodom Sihanouk Varman
King of Cambodia...
a much misunderstood monarch who deeply cares for his people.

CONTENTS

FOREWORD

By His Majesty
Preah Bat Samdech Preah
Norodom Sihanouk Varman
King of Cambodia

The heritage of the builders of Angkor has been abundantly documented since the temples were discovered by French explorer Henri Mouhot. However, not much has been written about the Royal Palace in Phnom Penh, a complex that shelters superb examples of Khmer architecture and art.

I am, therefore, delighted that my good friend H.E. Julio A. Jeldres, our Official Biographer, has taken the time to research and produce this timely album about our Royal Palace in Phnom Penh in order that our future generations and our foreign friends can have a better understanding of the traditional Khmer buildings and numerous pieces of art which over the years have found a home in the Royal Palace's complex.

The Royal Palace of Phnom Penh was built by my great-grandfather, His Majesty King Norodom, after he decided to leave the former royal capital of Oudong, in 1866, and established the capital in Phnom Penh. Our former Kings had initially lived in provisional quarters, built of wood and bamboo, to the north of the current Palace. In 1870, the Royal Palace was definitively installed at its current location but additional premises in stone replaced the former wooden structure of the Palace.

From 1915 to 1917, the construction of the "Preah Tineang Tevea Vinicchay" or "The august residence of God the Arbiter" took place, it included the current Throne Hall and other smaller buildings, always using the traditional Khmer architecture. The new premises were officially inaugurated by His Majesty King Sisowath on 16 May 1919. In 1932, my grandfather,

King Monivong presided over the construction of the Khemarin Palace, which has served as the residence of our previous Kings, including my parents King Norodom Suramarit and Queen Sisowath Kossomak and of visiting Heads of State such as General Charles de Gaulle of France, President Tito of Yugoslavia, Emperor Haile Selassie of Ethiopia, President Soeharto of Indonesia and many others.

After my restoration to the Cambodian Throne, in September 1993, Queen Monineath and I, we have arranged for the renovation of the visitors' quarters in the Khemarin Palace, the total renovation of the Sahametrei Hall, where my mother Queen Kossomak spent the last years of her life and of the gardens of the complex.

I sincerely appreciate the publication of this album about our Royal Palace and wish to thank all the persons that have contributed to its realisation. I am sure that this album will be largely successful with people interested in Cambodian history, the Cambodian monarchy and our traditional and unique Khmer architecture.

PREFACE

I became interested in Cambodia's rich cultural heritage back in 1967, when as a high school student in Chile, I read about Jacqueline Kennedy's visit to Cambodia. The visit had received worldwide coverage because people mistakenly believed that she was carrying a message from the President of the USA for the restoration of diplomatic relations with Cambodia, which had been broken off by the then Prince Norodom Sihanouk in 1965.

There was no such message and the USA's former First Lady was simply fulfilling a wish she had to visit Angkor. She was accorded a great welcome by Prince Sihanouk, who escorted her to an audience with the late Queen, Her Majesty Kossomak Nearireath.

I was impressed by Cambodian architecture and tried to find information in Chile about that country, but there was none. So, I wrote to the Cambodian Permanent Mission to the United Nations asking for some information and then I forgot about it. Four months later, a letter arrived from the Royal Palace in Phnom Penh. It was signed Norodom Sihanouk, Head of State.

My original letter had been forwarded by the Cambodian Mission in New York to the Royal Palace and Prince Sihanouk replied himself saying that he was pleased to learn that a Chilean student was interested in his country, so many miles away. He also said that he had instructed his secretariat to send me information about Cambodia.

In due course, I received a complete library about Cambodia, for which my mother had to pay a huge amount of money to the Chilean Post Office, prompting her to forbid me from writing again asking for information about foreign countries.

But it was too late, I had become fascinated by the personality of Norodom Sihanouk and continued to write to the Prince, who always made a point of replying to each of my letters. I also learned French in order to be able to use that language in my letters to the Prince.

I didn't realise at the time that a single letter would change my life forever and that soon I would leave Chile in search of Cambodia. I went on to study in Australia while keeping up my correspondence with the Prince, who had been forced by events to take up residence in Peking (now known as Beijing).

From April 1975, after the Khmers Rouges took over Cambodia, I lost contact with the Prince until February 1979, when he reappeared in New

York, following the Vietnamese invasion of Cambodia. We re-established our correspondence and soon afterwards I went to visit him and Princess Monique in Pyongyang, North Korea, where he was the guest of the late President Kim Il Sung.

Not long after that, I began helping him and moved to Bangkok to work at the office he had established in the Thai capital to rally the royalist elements struggling against the Vietnamese occupation of Cambodia. I became his Private Secretary and accompanied him during his visits to Asean countries and also to France and the United Nations. I remained his Private Secretary, Chief of Secretariat and Special Assistant until December 1991, when Sihanouk returned to Cambodia, as part of the Paris Agreements on Cambodia.

The idea of this book came about during a private audience with His Majesty in early February 1997. His Majesty had just hosted the state visit to Cambodia of then President Soeharto of Indonesia, and a member of the Indonesian delegation had asked whether there was a book available about the Royal Palace and its history.

I took up the idea of producing a book on the Royal Palace with enthusiasm and excitement. Little did I know what a difficult assignment it was going to be. I paid a visit to the National Archives in Phnom Penh where I was told that there was then little documentation on the construction of the Royal Palace in the archives that had already been sorted out, and that I would have to wait until new documents appeared in the processing of the archives, which were in a parlous state following Cambodia's years of war.

It was suggested to me that I may wish to travel to France and check the Archives d'Outre-Mer at Aix-en-Provence in the south of France, where many documents are kept from the period when Cambodia was a colony of France. The question was then to raise a budget allowing me to travel to France to undertake the necessary research.

My friends Michael and Kathleen Hayes, owners of the *Phnom Penh Post*, showed a distinct interest in the project from the beginning and decided to be the publisher of the book. They gave me a budget which allowed me to travel to France and also to return to Cambodia to conduct research and interviews.

His Excellency Gildas Le Lidec, the French Ambassador to Cambodia, and Michel Igout of the French Cultural Service, also took a keen interest in the project and were instrumental in opening doors for me during my visit to France in search of the documentation on the Royal Palace. I am most grateful to both of them.

Unfortunately, the political situation in Cambodia was not helpful to my project, and any potential sponsors that I approached declined because they were cutting expenditure. Things took a turn for the worse while I was in Aix-en-Provence in July 1997, where I learned that a coup had taken place in Phnom Penh and many people, including some friends of mine, had been killed.

I was shocked and sad. During a stopover in Bangkok, I met with Kathleen Hayes, who had more bad news. Because of events in Cambodia, they were forced to put the project on hold, as their financial commitments did not allow them to justify the expenditure on the book. I well understood Michael and Kathleen Hayes's dilemma and I wish to place on record here my sincere gratitude to them. Without their initial support, commitment and enthusiasm for the project, this book would have never been made possible.

I abandoned the project for some months, always keeping an alert eye for photos and documents about the Royal Palace of Phnom Penh, while waiting for the political situation in Cambodia to improve. As soon as the elections of July 1998 were over, I started work on the book again.

Documenting the construction and history of the Royal Palace of Phnom Penh has been made difficult by the lack of archives at the Royal Palace itself, where a researcher could check dates and events. I have thus relied on the assistance given me by the Director of Conservation of the Royal Palace—Chum Ngoeun, by his deputy Nou Horn, his staff and the guides of the Royal Palace, who kindly answered my questions whenever I needed to ascertain historical facts.

It should be pointed out here that their information does not come from any text available to them, but was passed on to them by former employees of the Royal Palace. For purposes of accuracy, I have checked their information with whatever other sources I was able to find.

His Majesty the King and Her Majesty the Queen have been most supportive of this project. His Majesty has personally taken time from his very hectic schedule to go through chapters of the book adding his own personal knowledge of the Royal Palace. I am indebted to Their Majesties for their kind support.

H.E. Laetitia van den Assum, Ambassador of the Netherlands to Cambodia, has been a very strong supporter of this project as well as a wonderful friend. She hosted me at her residence for four months while the main writing was being done. I am indebted to Ambassador van den Assum for her wonderful support.

Annelies Boogaerdt, Rob and Lucy Bosscher, and Yvonne van Bruchem of the Netherlands Embassy have also been very kind and helpful with this project. My sincere gratitude to them all.

I am indebted to the Embassy of the Federal Republic of Germany in Phnom Penh; the Royal Netherlands Embassy in Bangkok; the Ministry of Tourism of Cambodia; the Shell Company of Cambodia, Bangkok Airways, Raffles International, through its two hotels in Cambodia—Le Royal in Phnom Penh and the Grand Hotel d'Angkor in Siemreap; Air France; H.E. Ambassador Truong Mealy, former Cambodian Ambassador to Japan; H.E. Pou Sothirak, former Minister of Industry of the Royal Government of Cambodia; and H.E. Ambassador Fernando Gelbard, former Argentine Ambassador to France for their generous sponsorship, who also made publication of this book possible.

I would also like to thank the following people for their kind assistance with this project:

Dr. Withaya Sucharithanaragse, Director, and Suda Suntisaveekul of the Institute of Asian Studies, Chulalongkorn University, for the many facilities extended to me to conduct research for this book;

Jacques Nepote of the French National Centre for Research, whose important thesis on the Royal Palace of Phnom Penh still remains unpublished;

H.E. Nouth Narang, former Misnister of Culture of the Royal Government of Cambodia;

Diana MacKintosh, former Private Secretary to His Majesty the King, who has served as "liaison officer" in Paris and found many photos and documents on the Royal Palace for this book;

Peter Arfanis and the staff of the National Archives of Cambodia, for their help in searching documents about the Royal Palace of Phnom Penh;

Mme. Durand-Evrard, Director; Lucette Vachier and Serge Dubuisson and other staff of the Centre des Archives d'Outre Mer at Aix-en-Provence;

Louis Amigue, Director, and Isabelle Nathan of the Archives of the French Foreign Ministry;

Denys Lombard, Jean-Louis Taffarelli and Olivier de Bernon of the French School of the Far East;

Jeanne Beausoleil, Director, and Martine Ruby of the Musée Albert Kahn in Boulogne (France);

H.E. Kong Som Ol, Vice-prime minister and Minister of the Royal Palace, for facilitating the photography and documentation work through his staff;

My friends and colleagues at the Private Secretariat of His Majesty the King and in particular H.E. Oum Weakchiravuth, Deputy Chief of the Royal Secretariat; and H.E. Khek Sysoda, Minister-director of the Royal Protocol.

In Bangkok, I enjoyed the charming hospitality and humour of Cees Van Oye and Chanyuth Boochinda and more recently of André de Bussy.

In Paris, Marie-Paule Serre and her two sons opened their house to me and were helpful in finding documents from archives and libraries.

I am also grateful to the following for their encouragement, critical comments and ideas:

H.R.H. Samdech Preah Ream Norodom Buppha Devi; H.R.H. Princess Norodom Marie; Ambassador Roland Eng; Ambassador David Matnai of Israel; Ambassador Cesar Gonzalez-Palacios of Spain; Ambassador Lars Albert Wensell of Norway; Dominic Faulder; Serge Thion; Penny Edwards; Peter Bartu; Colin Pratt; Mara Moustafine; Madeleine de Langalerie; Marina Pok; Kem Bopha; Huoth Ravouth; Suon Sareth; Youk Chhang; Scott Rosenberg; Hann So; Kelvin So; Peter Schier; Narisa Thaitawat and Christian Guay.

Last but not least, my sincere gratitude goes to Nusara Thaitawat, one of Thailand's finest journalists, who has not only been a friend but has helped me to find sponsors and encouraged me when I was about to abandon the project. And to Noel Deschamps, former Australian Ambassador to Cambodia (1962-1969) who through his humility, friendship and wisdom has guided me through my activities for Cambodia and its people.

I have made every possible effort to produce a book that is entertaining and accurate. Any mistakes, particularly over dates and names, are obviously my own.

Southeast Asia

China

Myanmar

Laos

Hanoi

Hainan

Vientiane

Rangoon

Mekong River

Thailand

Bangkok

Tonle Sap

Cambodia

Phnom Penh

Vietnam

Gulf of Thailand

Andaman Sea

Ho Chi Minh City

South China Sea

Malaysia

Kuala Lumpur

Singapore

Indonesia

CAMBODIA'S HISTORY IN BRIEF

The historical origins of the Kingdom of Cambodia can be traced to the 1st and 6th centuries A.D. and to a pre-Angkorean Kingdom known as Funan. According to an ancient Cambodian legend, an Indian Brahman priest by the name of Kaundinya came to Cambodia's Great Lake to find fortune.

There, he met and married a local princess—Soma, daughter of the Naga king, also known as the "Lord of the Soil". Their marriage is said to have established the "Lunar Dynasty" of Funan, symbolising the fertility of the Kingdom and occupying a central place in Khmer cosmology. It is said that after the marriage was consummated, the Naga King, Soma's father, drank the flood waters of the Mekong, thus enabling the people to cultivate the land.

The Kingdom of Funan was a state based on Hindu customs, legal traditions and the Sanskrit language. Funan is said to have been initially established on the banks of the Mekong river by tribal people migrating from South China, probably from the province of Yunnan, in the middle of the 3rd century A.D., and it became the oldest Indianised state in Southeast Asia.

In the mid-6th century, Funan was taken over by the vassal state known as Chen-la. According to Khmer legends, Chen-la was the immediate predecessor of the Khmer Empire, which at its zenith extended to most of present Cambodia, parts of Vietnam, Laos, Thailand and the Malay peninsula.

The Khmer kings were able to marshal forces to build the most extensive complex of religious temples in the world, the Angkor complex, with Angkor Wat becoming the capital of the empire.

As the Angkor era came to an end, Cambodia's capital moved first to the south, to a place known as Lovek, and then to Oudong, not far from the current capital of Phnom Penh, to which King Norodom moved his court in 1865.

From the 17th century, Cambodia was under the influence of the Siamese Kingdom. The country was fought over by the expansionist Siamese and Vietnamese through the 17th and 18th centuries.

By the mid-1800s, Cambodia, like most other nations in Asia, was under pressure from European colonial expansion. King Ang Duong (1847-1859) resisted such pressure, unified the Kingdom and made substantial reforms to the administration. King Norodom (1860-1904) signed a Protectorate Treaty with the French which led to 90 years of French domination over the Khmer people.

King Norodom died in 1904 and was succeeded by his brother King Sisowath, who ruled Cambodia from 1904 to 1927 and was in turn succeeded by his son, King Monivong (1927-1941).

In 1941, the throne passed to a royal prince who belonged to both the Norodom and Sisowath branches of the Royal Family by virtue of the fact that his father was a Norodom and his mother a Sisowath. Prince Norodom Sihanouk was crowned King on 28 October 1941.

In 1953, King Sihanouk obtained independence from France and began the process of building a prosperous country, united and in peace. In 1955, King Sihanouk abdicated the throne in order to participate more fully in the political life of the country. His father, Norodom Suramarit, was elected King and Prince Sihanouk was elected to the newly created position of Head of State.

During the 1950s and 1960s Cambodia made successful advances in all fields of its national development. It became a substantial exporter of rubber and even managed a modest surplus of rice for export.

Unfortunately, the war raging in neighbouring Laos and Vietnam expanded to Cambodia in the late 1960s. And on 18 March 1970 Prince Sihanouk was overthrown in a foreign-sponsored coup d'état by General Lon Nol.

Sihanouk went to live in exile in China and became the leader of the anti-Lon Nol struggle. On 17 April 1975, the communist Khmers Rouges took over Cambodia and initially accepted Sihanouk as a figurehead of state. But as soon as Sihanouk realised that the regime was responsible for tremendous violations of human rights, he resigned and was then placed under house arrest until January 1979, when on the personal intervention of Chinese Vice-premier Deng Xiaoping, Sihanouk was flown to China and was asked to assume the leadership of the struggle against Vietnam's occupation of Cambodia.

Years of foreign occupation and civil war followed until October 1991 when a peace agreement was signed in Paris, allowing Sihanouk and other opposition leaders to return to Cambodia.

In 1993, a general election was held under United Nations supervision and a new National Assembly was elected, which proceeded to draft a new Constitution. Cambodia again became a monarchy and Prince Sihanouk was elected to reascend the throne he had abdicated in 1955.

The Royal Palace of Phnom Penh

W N E S

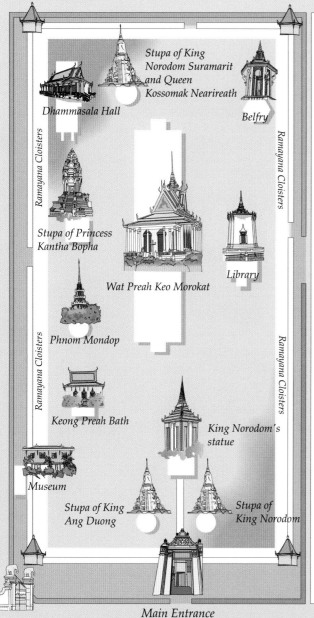

Stupa of King Norodom Suramarit and Queen Kossomak Nearireath

Dhammasala Hall

Belfry

Ramayana Cloisters

Stupa of Princess Kantha Bopha

Library

Wat Preah Keo Morokat

Phnom Mondop

Ramayana Cloisters

Ramayana Cloisters

Keong Preah Bath

King Norodom's statue

Museum

Stupa of King Ang Duong

Stupa of King Norodom

Main Entrance

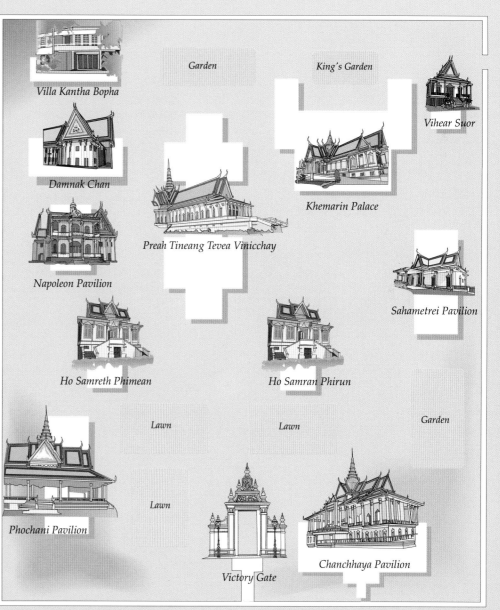

Villa Kantha Bopha

Garden

King's Garden

Vihear Suor

Damnak Chan

Khemarin Palace

Preah Tineang Tevea Vinicchay

Napoleon Pavilion

Sahametrei Pavilion

Ho Samreth Phimean

Ho Samran Phirun

Lawn

Lawn

Garden

Phochani Pavilion

Lawn

Victory Gate

Chanchhaya Pavilion

1806. CAMBODGE — Phnom-Penh — Vue du Palais Roy

INTRODUCTION

T he Royal Palace of Phnom Penh was established more than a century ago in the site chosen by a commission of royal astrologers and ministers, because it had the auspicious qualities necessary for the quarters of the king, who was regarded as a direct descendant of the Gods, living on earth under the influences of the forces of heaven.

The royal astrologers felt that the site where the four waterways converge had the perfect blend of the movements of the planets and the cycles of the seasons to make the living environment of the king peaceful, healthy and prosperous. The site is known as "Chaktomouk Mongkol" because it is located opposite where the waters of the Upper Mekong, the Lower Mekong, the Basak and Tonle Sap rivers converge.

The Royal Palace, built in 1866 during the French Protectorate (1847-1953) by Neak Okhna Tepnimith Mak, is similar to the Royal Grand Palace in Bangkok, but smaller. The Royal Palace in Phnom Penh differs, however, from that of Bangkok in its orientation which is to the East and not the North as in Bangkok.

Begun by King Norodom (1860-1904), King Sihanouk's great-grandfather, the Royal Palace has been extensively modified and remodelled by subsequent monarchs and at one time was both the administrative and religious centre of the Kingdom, as well as the formal residence of the king. From 1970 to 1991 the Royal Palace became a museum, maintained by the different regimes in power in Cambodia and parts of it deteriorated but were not renovated until after the Paris Peace Agreements on Cambodia were signed in October 1991.

Built in traditional Khmer architectureal and decorative style, the different buildings of the Royal Palace also have some Western features to make living and working conditions comfortable.

A view of the Royal Palace in the early 19th century with Wat Preah Keo Morokat at the left. The King's original residence which was replaced later on by the Khemarin Palace can be seen at the far right.

Location and history

THE ROYAL CHRONICLES mention that in 1434, King Ponhea Yat (1432-1467) had already chosen Phnom Penh as his capital. Other sources dispute this and suggest that Phnom Penh was chosen as capital in 1446, after the fall of Angkor, and remained as such until 1494. There is, however, no mention in the chronicles of a site being set apart for the construction of a residence for the king, nor are there any remains from the first royal construction, if ever there was one on this site.

Just as the old Khmer Empire moved its capital, in accordance with its strategic and defensive needs, from Angkor to Basan and then to Lovek, Cambodian sovereigns also moved their residences, starting with Phnom Penh, then to Oudong and finally again to Phnom Penh.

According to the royal chronicles, in 1813 after a Siamese attack King Ang Chan (1796-1834) established a citadel, known as the Cristal Citadel, on the same site as the current Palace. The citadel seems to have served as the king's provisional residence until December of the same year, when finding himself without any troops, the king withdrew to Vinhlong in Annam, seeking the support of the Annamese

The royal elephants rehearsing for a royal ceremony in front of the Royal Palace. The photo was taken in early 20th century.

Emperor against his domestic enemies. The citadel was destroyed by the Siamese in 1834 when they put the town to the torch.

The Palace, known by the locals as the "Village of the King" is a rather extensive enclosure, a city within a city, of approximately 500 metres by 800 metres. As already mentioned, all buildings, grounds and outbuildings are oriented towards the East.

External stone walls decorated with reproductions of the leaves of a traditional Khmer tree known as Seima provided security to the compound while internal walls separate the different courtyards and provide security and a calm environment for the sovereign. Smaller gates provide entrance from one courtyard to the next thus avoiding the need to go out through the east.

Most of the buildings in the compound have been built following the traditional layout of the buildings at Angkor, as modern Cambodians pride themselves on being descendants of the builders of Angkor. They therefore attached great importance to the architectural forms of the Palace.

For instance, the sovereign can only make a public appearance if his tribune is at a higher level than the audience. This explains the construction of the Chanchhaya Pavilion, from which the king can address the people below in the street. Similarly, in the Throne Hall the throne is raised to represent Mount Meru.

In Cambodia, as in the rest of Southeast Asia, palaces were built with three main purposes in mind. Firstly, as mentioned above, they should serve as the residence of the sovereign or ruler in a calm and peaceful environment. Secondly, the buildings should be functional enough to

The Royal Palace of Phnom Penh

allow the practice of the ancient court ceremonial. Finally, they were meant to be a symbol of the Kingdom, where the sovereign could receive other foreign kings and important visitors with dignity and honour.

In his book "The Land of the White Elephant", American traveller and writer Frank Vincent described his 1872 visit to the Royal Palace of Phnom Penh as follows:

"The Palace is but just completed. It was planned and its erection was superintended by a French architect, but it was built through out by Cambodian workmen. The construction and furnishing is thoroughly European in nearly every part. Entering at the grand central door, the hall leads directly to the reception room, and this opens into the parlour. Upon the right of these rooms is the dining-room, and upon the left the library, staircase, and billiard-room".

Admittedly, Vincent was referring here to the first royal residence built for King Norodom by the French Protectorate in the traditional European style. In 1931, under King Monivong (1927-1941), the old royal residence was pulled down and the Khemarin Palace was built. This has been the royal residence ever since.

But Vincent also pointed to the presence of traditional Khmer features in the buildings of the palace compound:

"Directly before the palace building is the private office of the King, a handsomely furnished little room where His Majesty receives all visitors

The Victory Gate—main entrance to the Royal Palace in 1918.

on business; behind it are the reception halls, in process of erection and nearly completed. These buildings, built of brick, with tiled roofs and gaily ornamented in the Siamese style, are quite imposing".

It should also be noted that in adopting Western features for his Palace, King Norodom wanted to make an effort to bring his country into a more modern era and to be seen as a monarch who was not afraid of Western ideas and influence.

Successive Cambodian monarchs have made sure that their palaces have been open to their people, keeping only the private apartments of the sovereign from the public eye. Already in 1872, Frank Vincent observed:

"We entered by a private side gate—for access to the palace enclosure may be had at all times".

French explorer Lucien Henry, who visited Cambodia in 1894, wrote:

"The palace is open to the whole world, only the private apartments of the monarch and the ladies' household are out of limits to the public. The children of Norodom also live within the Cambodian Elysée, which offers a vague impression of a city swarming with people".

Since the restoration of the monarchy in September 1993, Their Majesties King Norodom Sihanouk and Queen Norodom Monineath have paid much attention to maintaining and beautifying the buildings and gardens surrounding the palace, which were in a parlous state.

The guest quarters in the Khemarin Palace have been renovated and expanded and new gardens have been established behind the royal residence. The government of

Germany generously paid for the renovation and restoration of the roof of the Throne Hall.

Today, the Royal Palace remains the symbol of Cambodian royalty even though the rituals have evolved considerably with the passing of time. For many Cambodians, particularly those from the rural areas of the country, the "Village of the King" remains the place where they can go for help during times of need. They know they will not be turned away because royal tradition demands that the sovereign must always listen to his people's call for help.

(top right) A aerial view of the Throne Hall and the Khemarin Palace under construction.
(lower right) Royal Guards in the early 19th century.
(below) The six principal consorts of King Sisowath **(1940-1927)**.
(opposite page) Extensive construction of the Royal Palace were carried out during the reign of King Norodom **(1860-1940)**.

PHNOM-PENH — Groupe de Gardiens du Palais

PHOM-PENH — Les six favorites de Sa Majesté Sisowath

Significant Dates Related to the Construction of the Royal Palace of Phnom Penh

Reign of King Norodom (1860-1904)

Early 1863
• Provisional wooden palace built in Phnom Penh, north of Wat Unnalom.

11 August 1863
• Signature of Treaty with France.

3 June 1864
• Norodom is crowned King.

December 1865
• King Norodom leaves Oudong palace.

Early 1866
• The Royal Court is moved to the new palace known in the Khmer language as "Brah Parama Raja Vamn Bhak" or "The august enclosure in the surroundings of the Supreme King".

1867
• Capital established in Phnom Penh.

1869-1870
• Construction of the first (wooden) Throne Hall.

Late 1871
• Permanent installation of the Royal Court in the new premises.

1873
• Walls surrounding the palace are erected.

1876
• The Napoleon Pavilion, a gift from Emperor Napoleon III of France, is assembled within the complex.

Reign of King Sisowath (1904-1927)

27 April 1906
• King Sisowath succeeds his elder brother.

1 January 1907
• Establishment within the palace complex of "Manufacture Royale".

1907
• Construction of the Phochani Hall (the Banquet Hall).

1910
• Demolition of several houses in the complex, including the house occupied by the Minister of the Palace.

10 September 1912
• Inauguration of the Phochani Hall .

1912/1913
• Demolition of the old Chanchhaya Pavilion.

9 January 1914
• Inauguration of the new Chanchhaya Pavilion.

1914/1915
• Demolition of the old Throne Hall.

26 July 1915
• Construction of new Throne Hall begins.

1917/1918
• Demolition of old premises surrounding the Throne Hall.

1918
• Construction of two lateral pavilions, on either side of the entrance of the Throne Hall.

16 May 1919:
• Inauguration of the Throne Hall.

1920
• Transfer of the King's Elephants to the south of the Wat Preah Keo Morokat.

Reign of King Monivong (1927-1941)

1930
• Construction of the Royal Chapel (Vihear Suor)

24 June 1931
• Construction of the Khemarin Palace, current residence of the Cambodian sovereign, begins.

1st Reign of King Norodom Sihanouk (1941-1955)

1941
• Establishment of the Palace Museum. European-style kitchen added to Khemarin Palace.

1953
• Construction of Damnak Chan.
• Construction of the Villa Kantha Bopha.

Reign of King Norodom Suramarit (1955-1960)

17 September 1956
• Inauguration of the Villa Kantha Bopha, a residence for visiting foreign heads of state.

22 September 1956
• Inauguration of the building for the High Council of the Throne.

1960
• Constructions of the stupa of H.M. King Norodom Suramarit.

1962
• Renovation of Wat Preah Keo Morokat.

2nd Reign of King Norodom Sihanouk (25 September 1993)

1994
• Restoration of the roof of the Throne Hall, funded by the Federal Republic of Germany.
• Complete restoration of the Sahametrei Pavilion.
• Renovation of Damnak Chan which becomes officially the Preah Reach Damnak Preah Kossomak.

1994/1995
• Complete restoration of the old gardens of the Palace and new ones added.

1995
• Refurbishing of the guest quarters of the Khemarin Palace.
• Refurbishing of the Elephant Museum.

1997
• Renovation of the Villa Kantha Bopha.

WAT PREAH KEO MOROKAT

W at Preah Keo Morokat literally means the Temple of the Emerald Buddha. The temple, also known as the Silver Pagoda, was built between the years 1892 and 1902 and was renovated for the first time in 1962. Further renovations particularly to the murals of the walls surrounding the temple were done by Polish specialists between 1985 and 1988.

Built in the traditional style of Khmer architecture, the temple was formerly known as the temple of Ubosoth Rathanaram. Ubosoth is a word that comes from the ancient Pali and describes the practice of the Lord Buddha's eight precepts which are:

1. Not to kill
2. Not to steal
3. Not to commit adultery
4. Not to lie, slander, gossip or use harsh speech
5. Not to drink alcohol
6. Not to eat at the wrong time of day
7. Not to dance, sing, play music or watch entertainments
8. Not to use personal adornments such as cosmetics

The temple was initially constructed in wood and brick during the reign of King Norodom. It was first open for the

Wat Preah Keo Morokat facing the Northwest as seen in a photograph taken in the early 20th century.

BODGE - Phnom-Penh -- Pagode royale face Nord-Est

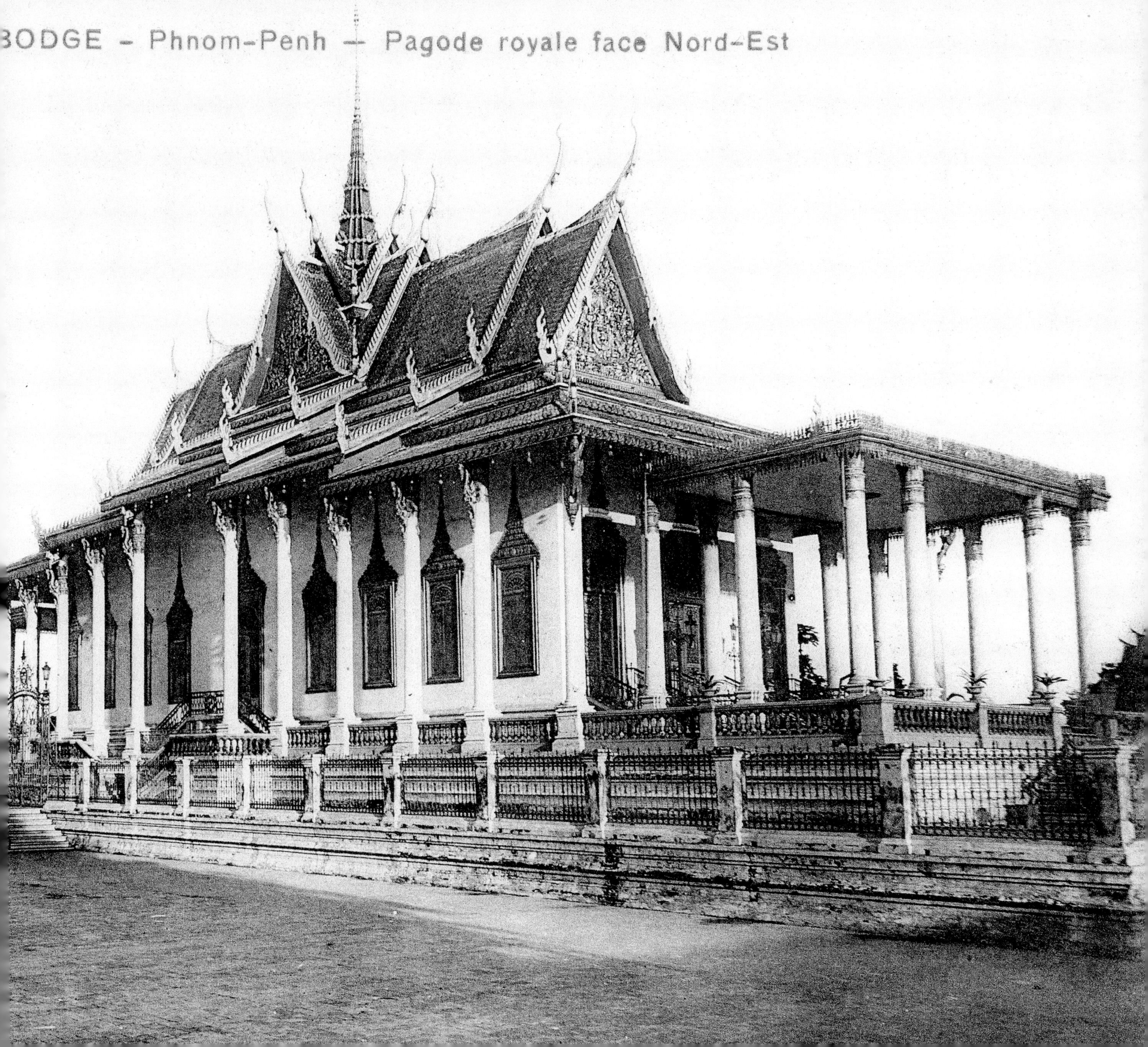

"Seima Festival", a Buddhist festival during which a monument known as a "Seima" is erected near the temple. The festival normally takes place on the eighth day of the waxing of the moon of the third month of the lunar calendar, corresponding to January-February. Accordingly some reports suggest that the first Seima Festival at the Temple of the Emerald Buddha fell on Thursday, 5 February 1903 and that the ceremonies were presided over by the King himself to mark completion of the building of the temple.

Successive Khmer monarchs used the temple as a chapel to listen to sermons given by Buddhist monks on how to follow the practice of Ubosoth. They also came to the temple for ceremonies to venerate and bless the Emerald Buddha kept in the temple or simply to engage in meditation in order to develop a peaceful mind, in particular during Buddhist festivals.

Wat Preah Keo Morokat has also been used by the Royal Family and members of the Court to perform royal ceremonies throughout the year according to Buddhist traditions.

(left) Prince Narindrapong and Prince Sihamoni carry the ashes of their grandmother—the late Queen Kossomak Nearireath—for burial in the Royal Palace's grounds in September 1975. Also present are Their Majesties the King and Queen and three Khmer Rouge leaders (from left) Hu Nim, Son Sen and Khieu Samphan. (above) Garudas supporting the temple roof structure are believed to keep the bad spirits away.

(above) Another view of Wat Preah Keo Morokat.
(right) Exquisite designs of the pediment at the back entrance.
(far right) Details on the doors of Wat Preah Keo Morokat.

Wat Preah Keo Morokat

The Royal Palace of Phnom Penh

The temple differs from other Buddhist pagodas because monks do not reside within its premises. His Majesty King Norodom Sihanouk resided at the temple for three months during his royal ordination which began on 31 July 1947.

It has been a tradition that every time the monarchs wish to celebrate a ceremony at Wat Preah Keo Morokat they would invite monks from other pagodas such as Botum Vadei or Unnalom, pagodas located in the centre of Phnom Penh, to come to Wat Preah Keo Morokat to participate in the royal ceremonies.

However, the weather and age contributed to the gradual deterioration of the fabric of the temple, to the point of near collapse and the need for urgent repairs. In 1962, Queen Kossomak Nearireath, the Mother of King Norodom Sihanouk, approved plans for the construction of a new temple built in concrete. The new structure was built in the same place as the old wood and brick one, using the same architectural style. Marble was imported from Italy to cover the terrace and columns of the new temple.

(above) A Khmer-style lion guarding the entrance to the Mondop canopy sheltering the King Norodom's Statue (seen in the background).
(left) Delicate decorations on the roof of the Mondop canopy. (opposite page) An imposing view of the Temple of the Emerald Buddha.

The temple is known as the "Temple of the Emerald Buddha" because it houses a Buddha image made of emerald. It is also known, mainly by foreigners, as the "Silver Pagoda" because of the 5,329 silver tiles that cover the floor of the temple. Each tile weighs 1,125 grams and all of them were individually handcrafted by Khmer silversmiths.

Within the temple there are 1,650 artifacts, comprising Buddhist statues made of a variety of precious metals such as gold, silver and bronze, with diamonds, sapphires, rubies and other precious stones inlaid. Many of these artifacts were presented to the temple by members of the Royal Family. Senior officials from the Cambodian government and wealthy Cambodians have also donated religious artifacts to the temple.

Inside the main hall stands a statue of a Buddha known as the "Buddha of the Future" or "Buddha Maitreya". This statue is made of solid gold and weighs 90 kilogrammes including the stand and parasol. The statue also has 2,086 diamonds, the largest of which, located on the Buddha's crown,

(above) The Emeral Buddha in the main hall of the Wat Preah Keo Morokat.
(right) The main gate to Wat Preah Keo Morokat bearing King Norodom's royal insignia.
(opposite page) The main hall of the Wat Preah Keo Morokat.

The Royal Palace of Phnom Penh

weighs 25 karats. A smaller diamond of 20 karats is located in the Buddha's chest.

This Buddha statue was melted by King Sisowath in 1904 to comply with the will of his elder brother King Norodom, who had requested that after his cremation ceremony King Sisowath should melt his solid gold urn in order to make a statue representing the Buddha Maitreya. According to Buddhist traditions, King Norodom will be reincarnated as the Buddha Maitreya in the year 5000 of the Buddhist era (A.D. 4457). The statue was given the name of Preah Chinreangsei Reachika Norodom.

In the pavilion inside the main hall—known as Bossabok because of the roof with spire—which houses the Emerald Buddha there is also a small glass case where a sacred relic of the Buddha is preserved in a silver and gold stupa. The relic was brought from Sri Lanka by a monk named Lovea Em who lived in the Wat Langka pagoda in Phnom Penh.

Another case displays the offerings made by the late Queen Kossomak Nearireath, Mother of King Norodom Sihanouk. Donated to the temple in 1969, they consist mainly of statues made of gold depicting the life of the Buddha.

In former times the Khmer people followed two great religions: Brahmanism and Buddhism. These two religions originated from India and possess their own representative images which can be found throughout Cambodia, where Khmer sculptors adapted them to incorporate traditional Khmer characteristics.

(right) The solid gold statue of Buddha Maitreya. (opposite page, far left) Main street entrance to the Wat Preah Keo Morokat complex; (top and lower left) East meets West in the wooden windows at the Temple of the Emerald Buddha. (lower right) Seima adorns at the base of the temple building.

Cambodian scholars researching the establishment of both religions in Cambodia believe that the creation of the Buddhist statues took place after the Lord Buddha's Nirvana more than 2,500 years ago. However, the scholars have been unable to find any statues dating from the period of the Lord Buddha's lifetime. Most of the statues were made in Gandhara city under the reign of King Kaniska from the fourth year of the Buddhist era.

In other display cases in the main hall, jewellery and silverware donated to the temple can be seen, as well as artifacts, mostly of gold and silver, used for religious ceremonies.

In the southern part of the temple there is a shrine known as Keong Preah Bath, where the footprints of the first four Buddhas believed to have reached Enlightenment are housed. These four Buddhas are named Kok Santho, Neak Komano, Kassapa and Gutama.

(left) Some of the precious Buddha statues in Wat Preah Keo Morokat.
(above) Keong Preah Bath (top) where the footprints of the first four Buddhas (lower) are enshrined.
(opposite page) The bustle of the street in front of the Temple's main entrance.

The Royal Palace of Phnom Penh

The Ramayana Cloisters

THE TEMPLE OF THE EMERALD BUDDHA is located in the southern section of the Royal Palace complex, enclosed by high cloisters. These cloisters were used as contemporary classrooms for Buddhist monks studying Pali before the Institute of Pali Language was established in Phnom Penh in 1930.

The walls of the cloisters are covered with mural frescos illustrating the Khmer version or "Ream Ker" of the Hindu Ramayana epic from beginning to end. The mural frescos were painted between 1903 and 1904 by well-known Khmer artists under the guidance of the painter and architect Oknha Tep Nimit Theak, assisted by the painter Vichitre Chea and a team of forty students.

The Ramayana epic frescos begin in the southernmost part of the eastern gallery and stretch around 604 metres of wall, reaching a height of 3.56 metres. They are the tallest mural frescos in Southeast Asia. On an area of 2,000 square metres, the exploits of the God Rama and of Lakshmana are shown with their army of monkeys making war against Ravana, an evil genius who has taken Rama's wife Sita.

(above) A main door leading to the Ramayana cloisters which boast the tallest mural frescos in Southeast Asia.
(opposite page, top) An old postcard showing the covered passage in early 19th century compared to a recent photograph of the same area (lower left). (lower right) A scene from Ramayana.

THE REAM KER

THE RAMAYANA or "The Glory of Rama" is an epic common to most countries in Southeast Asia where Buddhism has flourished. There are versions of the Ramayana in Burma, Cambodia, Laos, Indonesia and Thailand. Each country has its own particular version but the theme is the same and originates from India.

The version that has survived in Cambodia contains only some of the events of the original Indian version, and these have been changed to fit into a Theravada Buddhist frame of reference and into the Khmer language. Known in Cambodia as the Ream Ker, it remains the favourite epic of all Cambodians.

In modern times, the Cambodian Royal Ballet has incorporated into its repertoire selected episodes of the Ream Ker to be shown to distinguished guests visiting Cambodia, but there is also a popular version which has been staged at village festivals throughout the country.

The Ream Ker frescos of Wat Preah Keo Morokat as witnesses of the past are also substantial archives of information. They are the only easily accessible source presenting the Ramayana epic in lengthy detail, although the subject is also often presented as shadow theatre by the Royal Ballet, as well as being seen in sculptures and mural paintings in temples and pagodas around Cambodia since the time of the Khmer Empire. All these versions in various media constitute a rich and priceless heritage and a resource for students of ancient Khmer literature, culture, art and traditions.

The Royal Palace of Phnom Penh

Unfortunately, the weather and micro-organisms have gradually eroded the paintings. In October 1985 the Cambodian government therefore signed an agreement with the Directorate of State Enterprises of Poland, enabling Polish specialists to set up a project to preserve and restore the damaged frescos. From 1985 to 1992, these Polish specialists worked on repairing and renovating the paintings, as well as training Cambodian specialists in Poland on the techniques used for this work.

The Ream Ker in Brief

The epic relates how Prince Ream (Rama), eldest son of Dasaratha, King of Ayutthaya, capital of the Kingdom, following a promise made to his second wife Kaikesi, is deprived of his rights to the succession and condemned to exile. Followed by his wife, Sita and his younger brother Leak (Lakshmana), he vanishes into the forest haunted by demons.

Prince Reab (Ravana), King of the demons (or Rakshasas), falls in love with the beautiful Sita, kidnaps her and takes her as hostage to his palace in Langka. Aided by the prince of the monkeys, Hanuman, Prince Ream attacks Langka. There follows a merciless war between the two camps, representing good and evil, from which Prince Ream finally emerges as the victor.

Prince Ream liberates Sita but is doubtful of her fidelity. She demands to be allowed to walk on fire to prove her innocence. Prince Ream reconciles with Sita and returns to Ayutthaya, where he is crowned King.

Wat Preah Keo Morokat

King Norodom's Statue

IN FRONT OF the temple stand two stupas and a statue of King Norodom enshrined under a square structure with a pyramid-shaped pointed roof.

The statue is that of King Norodom on a horse. Created by the French sculptor Eude, it was completed in Paris in 1875. Initially located in a small garden on the river bank, it was transferred to the front of the Temple of the Emerald Buddha in 1892. King Norodom Sihanouk ordered the Mondop canopy built in 1953 as he embarked on his "Royal Crusade" to obtain Cambodia's full independence from France.

During this period the King came often to pray at the royal statue for victory against French colonialism. When Cambodia achieved independence, on 9 November 1953, King Sihanouk had the Mondop canopy built to cover the royal statue of his great-grandfather as a sign of gratitude towards King Norodom's sacred powers which had helped King Norodom Sihanouk to obtain the Cambodian people's freedom from French colonialism.

On each side of King Norodom's statue there are two stupas, one containing the ashes of King Ang Duong and the other the ashes of King Norodom.

Phnom Mondop

NOT FAR FROM Keong Preah Bath there is an artificial hill which symbolises Mount Kailasa. Here is where the Buddha is said to have made his own footprint in stone. The structure sheltering the Buddha's Footprint is decorated with 108 small statues that represent Lord Buddha's 108 past lives before he eventually reincarnated as Prince Siddharta and gained Enlightenment.

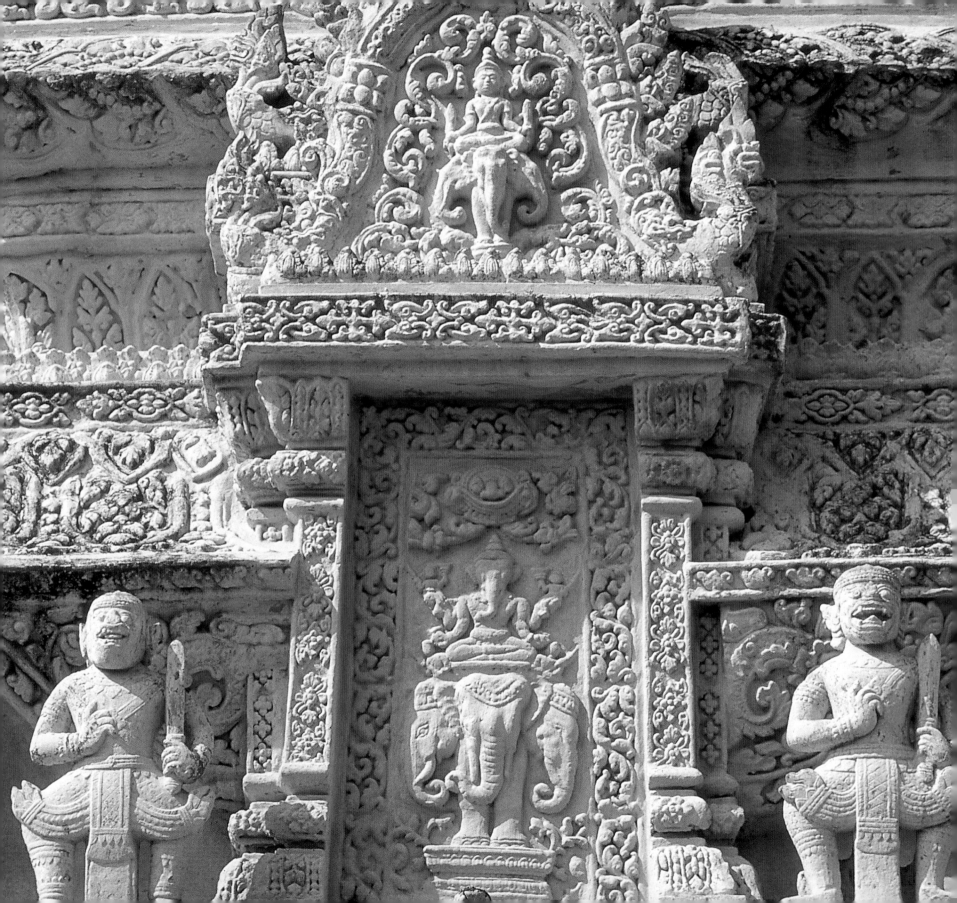

The Royal Stupas

THE SOUTHERN STUPA contains the cremated ashes of King Ang Duong and was built in 1908. King Ang Duong was the great-great-grandfather of His Majesty King Norodom Sihanouk.

The Northern Stupa contains the ashes of King Norodom and was also built in 1908. King Norodom was the great-grandfather of the present Monarch.

In the southern part of the temple there is also the Kantha Bopha sanctuary commemorating H.R.H. Princess Norodom Kantha Bopha, the favourite daughter of King Norodom Sihanouk who died of leukaemia at the age of four in 1952. The sanctuary was built in 1960 by the King to commemorate his daughter and was designed in the traditional form of a Khmer monument with carved decorations similar to those in the Independence Monument in Phnom Penh, but on a smaller scale.

A further stupa, at the extreme south of the temple, contains the ashes both of King Norodom Suramarit and Queen Kossomak Nearireath, parents of the current Monarch. King Norodom Suramarit died in 1960 and Queen Kossomak Nearireath in 1975.

(top right) Stupa containing the ashes of King Ang Duong.
(lower right) Sanctuary of H.R.H. Princess Kantha Bopha, daughter of H.M. King Norodom Sihanouk.
(opposite page) A closer view of the stuccoed reliefs that decorate the stupa of King Ang Duong.

The Belfry

THE BELL TOWER was rung as a sign to open or close the doors of the temple for ceremonies or to summon monks to classes in the cloisters surrounding the temple. The Bell Tower is located on the northwest side of the temple. According to the practices of Buddhism, every temple must also have a belfry to alert monks and lay people to the time for ceremonies or prayers.

As Wat Preah Keo Morokat does not have monks residing within its compound, the Belfry has not been used very much, but its presence is still necessary, to comply with Buddhist practices.

Dhammasala Hall

THE DHAMMASALA HALL, also in the southern area of the temple, is where Buddhist monks recite sacred texts for the well-being, health and longevity of the Royal Family of Cambodia. Nowadays, the hall is used by the Royal Family for receiving farmers and other people requiring assistance.

Wat Preah Keo Morokat

The Library

FINALLY, the Temple's Library, located on the north side, is one of the most important buildings in the precincts of the Temple of the Emerald Buddha, particularly for its contents. In effect the Library houses the Buddha's Tripitaka or "Three Baskets" which are the three collections of sacred Buddhist writings consisting of the Vinayapitaka, the Suttapitaka and the Abhidhamapitaka.

The Vinayapitaka is the collection of Buddhist texts describing disciplines and consisting of a series of instructions for monks;

The Suttapitaka is a collection of the teachings of the Buddha which explain what Buddhists should do and what they should not do, what is right and what is wrong;

The Abhidhamapitaka is a collection of Buddhist tests that explain the conception of mental activities, including suffering, happiness and the achievement of Nirvana.

The Buddha's Tripitaka consists of 110 volumes divided into 84,000 units.

Inside the Library building there is a statue of a sacred bull known as Nandin. This statue, believed to be very old, was found in Kohthom district of Kandal Province, in 1983. The statue is 80% silver and 20% other metals such as copper, iron, lead and zinc.

(far right) The sacred bull, Nandin, amidst worshipper's offerings. (right) Western-style stained glasses adorn the door frame of the Library.

Buddha Statues in Wat Preah Keo Morokat

• Abhaya Mudra (Gesture of Protection or Absence of Fear)

This gesture refers to the Buddha giving his sacred sermons to save the lives of human beings and teaching his disciples the ways to dispel fear. The Buddha stands with his right hand held up to execute the Abhaya Mudra, while the left hand hangs at his side.

• Vara Mudra (Gesture of Charity)

The Buddha stands with both hands hanging down at the sides and the palms of the open hands facing forwards. This Buddha figure can be seen both in the position of standing and sitting cross-legged.

• Vara Mudra II (Gesture of Expounding)

The Buddha's two open hands face forward with his middle figure folded against his thumb.

• Vara Mudra III (Gesture of Turning the Wheel of the Law)

The Buddha sits cross-legged with the fingers of each hand forming a wheel and placed against his chest. This gesture is seldom found in Buddha statues in Cambodia.

• Niyana Mudra (Gesture of Meditation)

The Buddha sits cross-legged, with both palms facing upwards on his lap.

• Bhumisparca Mudra (Gesture of Calling the Earth to Witness)

The Buddha sits cross-legged, his open right hand pointing towards the ground so as to call the Earth to witness, while his left hand remains open upward on his lap.

• Jatradana Mudra (Gesture of Asking for Alms)

The Buddha stands and holds his alms bowl. This represents the time for him to ask for alms from Buddhists.

• Sayana Mudra (Reclining Buddha)

The Buddha sleeps on his right side with his left hand resting on his side.

• Buddha Sheltered by the Naga

While the Lord Buddha was meditating close to the Muchalinda water-pond, there was a heavy rainfall during which the sacred Naga appeared, allowing the Buddha to sit on his coils and spreading his head over the Buddha to prevent him from getting wet. This kind of image of the Buddha is found frequently in Cambodia and other Buddhist countries.

• Buddha in Decoration

This figure is in the form of the King of the Universe wearing a crown, waist-belt and ring.

• Buddha in Gesture of Martyrdom

This image depicts a thin, rather bony Buddha, who has refused to eat while seeking to achieve Enlightenment.

PREAH TINEANG
TEVEA VINICCHAY

The Preah Tineang Tevea Vinicchay or the Throne Hall is the main building immediately opposite the Victory Gate and facing East. It was built in 1917 in the traditional Khmer style. Designed in the shape of a Roman cross, the Throne Hall is about sixty metres long and thirty metres wide, standing on a high base of approximately seven metres which constitutes a kind of ground floor, where space for offices and storage was once provided.

The Throne Hall has a tiered roof, covered in the traditional orange and green tiles, and a 59-metre spire which is said to have been influenced by the Bayon Temple in Angkor Wat.

The Throne Hall is where royal coronations, audiences for the prime minister, senior ministers and other state ceremonies traditional to the Cambodian monarchy, are held. It is also used for the formal reception and presentation of credentials of foreign envoys to the king.

The old all-wood Throne Hall before it was replaced by the current building in 1917.

Access to the Throne Hall is provided by a large brick and cement stairway edged with sculpted Nagas (water serpents with many mythological associations used as guardian figures) leading to the principal entrance of the hall. A covered terrace surrounds the hall, while Khmer-style columns adorned with Garudas (half-man, half-bird mythological figures) and Kinnaris (mythical figures with the head and chest of a female and the body of a bird) support the tiered roof.

(right) Napoleon Pavilion's western-style dome blends in with the Throne Hall's Khmer-style spired roof and Damnak Chan's tiered roof. (far right) The corners of the Throne Hall's roof are adorned with Garudas. (below) Preparation for King Monivong's Ceremonial Bath in 1928. (opposite page) Side view of the Throne Hall.

(top) The ceilings of the Throne Hall, embellished with magnificent frescos from the Ramayana.
(bottom) Majestic views inside the Throne Hall.
(left) The Throne and the Great White Umbrella—the symbol of kingship.

The Royal Palace of Phnom Penh

The ceilings of the Throne Hall are adorned, like the cloisters of the Wat Preah Keo Morokat, with superb frescos of the Khmer version of the Ramayana, the Ream Ker.

In 1994, the Federal Republic of Germany granted US$90,000 towards the restoration of the roof of the Throne Hall.

The Reach Balaing (the Throne) is the symbol of Cambodia's monarchy founded in the first century of the Christian era. The Reach Balaing is a square seat, intricately carved in precious wood and gilded. Garudas and Devas (celestial creatures inhabiting the lower levels of the Buddhist heaven) surround the base of the throne. It stands on an elevated dais, again representing Mount Meru.

Behind the Reach Balaing stands the Preah Tineang Bossobok, an open boat-shaped throne, carved and gilded, with a tapering spired roof, resting on elaborately gilded masonry and also surrounded by Deva figures in wood. Three stylised and superposed Nagas decorate

(above and left) The Preah Tineang Bossobok, an open boat-shaped throne with a towering spired roof, situated right behind the throne.

Preah Tineang Tevea Vinicchay

the base of the Bossobok, recalling the legendary origin of the Cambodian monarchy.

Between the Reach Balaing and the Preah Tineang Bossobok is a small reception area where private meetings between the King and visiting heads of state can take place on special occasions.

In the area just in front of the Preah Tineang Bossobok, gold-plated bronze busts of the five last kings and of Queen Kossamak Nearireath are displayed on wooden stands.

There are two smalls chapels inside the Throne Hall to the right and left of the throne. The chapel to the right, known as Ho Preah Athi (or Pavilion of the August Bones) houses gold and silver urns containing ashes of the five last Cambodian monarchs—King Ang Duong, King Norodom, King Sisowath, King Monivong and King Norodom Suramarit.

The other chapel, known as Ho Preah (or Pavilion of the August Buddha), to the left, houses many different Buddha images, property of the Cambodian monarchy. Because of their age, quality and the precious metals used in their making, some of these are of incalculable value.

On each side of the throne stands a statue of a deceased monarch:

To the right, a statue of King Sisowath (1904-1927) cast in copper and gold-plated by French sculptor P. Decuing in 1924; to the left, a statue of King Monivong, done by the same sculptor in 1936, also cast in copper and gold-plated.

**(top) Gold-plated bronze busts of Cambodia's past monarchs.
(bottom) The Royal regalia comprises the Betel Nut Set, the Receptacle, the Water Urn and the Libation Vessel— all in gold.**

Preah Moha Monti

LIKE ALL the buildings in the Royal Palace, the Throne Hall has a public area and a private one, where the monarch receives members of the Royal Family or change costumes between ceremonies. The Preah Moha Monti is equipped with all the necessary furnishings for the monarch's overnight stay if required. The Preah Moha Monti is also where the funeral urn containing the remains of a deceased monarch is kept until the cremation ceremony.

A beautifully-crafted royal bed to accommodate a king's overnight stay in Preah Moha Monti, no longer in use.

© Ambassador R. Eng

Priceless gifts from foreign heads of state are kept in the Ho Samran Phirun —now the Preah Sihanouk Museum.

Ho Samran Phirun

IMMEDIATELY TO the north side of the Throne Hall, there is a small pavilion known as the Ho Samran Phirun or "the pavilion where one sleeps in peace". This single storey pavilion was used by the king to take a rest, after the monarch had been travelling in the countryside on the back of a royal elephant.

Since 1997, the pavilion has become the Preah Sihanouk Museum, displaying gifts presented to His Majesty King Norodom Sihanouk by foreign heads of state.

Ho Samreth Phimean

LOCATED ON the south side of the Throne Hall is another small pavilion identical to Ho Samran Phirun. The building is known as Ho Samreth Phimean or "the Bronze Palace". The attributes of the royalty, the Sacred Sword, the Great Crown of Victory, the Victory Spear, the Fan and the Slippers had been kept here and guarded by the Bakus, the Brahman priests attached to the sovereign's court, since the first century of the Khmer monarchy.

Preah Tineang Tevea Vinicchay

The Victory Gate

THE VICTORY GATE is the principal entrance to the Royal Palace of Phnom Penh. It is flanked by two iron street lamps, unusual for such a place. The Gate is oriented towards the East and located in a splendid site, the main entrance to the Palace, opposite the Throne Hall.

Through the Victory Gate, foreign envoys enter the Palace when presenting their credentials to the King at the Throne Hall.

King Monivong seated on the throne the day of his Coronation in 1928.

CAMBODIAN ROYAL REGALIA

THE ROYAL REGALIA together with the Cambodian court's ceremonial items are essential parts of the Cambodian monarchy, which give stature to the office and bring home to the people the high respect accorded to the Cambodian sovereign.

Among the ancient items of the Cambodian Royal Regalia which were used in former times, we find the following: The Preah Moha Mokot Reach (The Great Crown of Victory), The Preah Moha Svetrachhatr (The Great White Umbrella of State), The Preah Khan Reach (The Sacred Sword), The Preah Lompeng Chey (The Victory Spear), The Preah Soporbatea (The Slippers), The Kriss, The Preah Veal Vichani (The Fan) and The Betel Nut Set, The Receptacle, The Water Urn and The Libation Vessel.

• The Preah Moha Mokot Reach

The Great Crown of Victory is the royal crown worn by all Cambodian sovereigns since the time of the Angkor empire. As shown in the reliefs of Angkor Wat, this kind of multi-tiered cone culminating in a tapering spire—symbol of the sacred mountain Preah Meru, and made of solid gold and precious stones, was worn by the sovereign for important state ceremonies.

• The Preah Moha Svetrachhatr

The Great White Umbrella of State is a nine-tiered white silk umbrella with gold thread which stands behind the throne. The tiers indicate the person's rank. In the past, in Cambodia, the Uparaja or Deputy King used a five-tiered umbrella and the King himself prior to his coronation used one of seven tiers, switching to a nine-tiered umbrella after the coronation. Similar umbrellas are found in Burma, Java and Thailand. They are said to be of Indian origin, where it appears the umbrella had greater importance than the crown itself.

• The Preah Khan Reach

The Sacred Sword is considered to be the "Safeguard of the Kingdom" and was kept in a small pavilion called "Pavilion of the Sacred Sword" within the Royal Palace near the Throne Hall, under the care of the court Brahmans, known as the "Bakus", who are the descendants of chaplains from the Angkorean era.

The sword is reported to have been crafted by Vishnu and Shiva in the A.D. 70 at the request of the God Indra, in order to be entrusted to the first Khmer king to ensure prosperity of his kingdom.

The French scholar Georges Groslier wrote in his book: Research on the Cambodians, *"Because of its decor, I date this weapon as being from the neo-Angkorean period and I would not be surprised if this is the same sword about which Chinese envoy Chou Ta-Kuan wrote in the 13th century".*

However, the sword's existence was only confirmed in the 16th century and the costumes of the figures decorating its sheath appear to indicate that it could not have been crafted before then.

The blade, inlaid with gold and silver, was regularly checked by the Bakus of the Royal Palace, who were in charge of its safety. Should the blade show any traces of rust, evoking the colour of blood. It was interpreted as being a disastrous omen for the country.

The Sacred Sword left its pavilion on only on one occasion—for the coronation of a new Cambodian king. The Sword and the Preah Moha Mokot Reach (Great Crown of Victory) were the principal insignia of Cambodia's royalty.

Following a Siamese invasion in 1783, the Preah Khan Reach was taken away to Bangkok. It was solemnly given back to Cambodia in 1864, on the occasion of the coronation of King Norodom.

King Rama I of Siam ordered the creation of a sword similar to the Cambodian one for use by the Siamese monarch. It was first used in his own coronation in 1785.

Photo courtesy: H.M. the King

The newly crowned King Norodom Sihanouk prepares for a horse ride within the grounds of the Royal palace.

The Preah Khan Reach, together with all other items of the Cambodian Royal Regalia disappeared from the Royal Palace in Phnom Penh immediately after the coup d'état of 18 March 1970, never to be seen again.

• The Preah Lompeng Chey

The August Victory Spear, also known as the Preah Seng Asorey, was always found together with the Sacred Sword. It is said that it also dates from the same Angkorean period.

An old Cambodian tale relates the story of the Victory Spear as follows:
"A poor farmer of the ethnic minority known as 'Samre' had specialised in the cultivation of sweet cucumber, whose seeds he had received in a supernatural fashion. He presented his first harvest to the King, who found the fruits so delicious that he made sure he had the exclusive right to them, giving instructions to the farmer to kill any intruders in his orchard, whether humans or animals.

It happened that during the rainy season, when cucumbers become scarce, the King being impatient to taste some, went himself to the orchard late at night and having been taken for an intruder by the farmer, was thus mortally wounded by the farmer's spear, with which the farmer defended his orchard and was subsequently buried as an intruder in the orchard.

As the King did not have a direct descendant and the dignitaries of the Kingdom were unable to agree on a successor, they decided to leave the matter of the succession to divine intervention through the action of the 'Elephant of Victory'. The great beast went and stood in front of the farmer, grower of the sweet cucumbers, and proceeded to greet him with his trunk between his legs, then knelt and gently wound his trunk round the farmer and placed him on his back. The farmer was duly anointed King."

The Victory Spear, which used to be kept in the Royal Palace next to the Sacred Sword, could have had the same age as the sword, because the style of the drawings and the pattern of the decorations of the two arms were identical.

The Victory Spear was cast in iron. The case bears gilt designs and the blade bears embossed or carved motifs at the base. Among these fine reliefs we can distinguish the mythical bird Garuda on a horse, set between four dragons' heads which form a kind of frame.

• The Preah Soporbatea

The slippers or flat shoes made of gold are very heavy and therefore only used during the coronation ceremony. Both in ancient Cambodia and Thailand shoes were regarded as being suitable only for royalty.

© Collection Léon Busy, Musée Albert Kahn

The Preah Khan Reach and the Preah Lompeng Chey had been kept in Ho Samreth Phimean before they disappeared from the Palace in 1970.

• The Kriss

The Kriss has also a history that is difficult to authenticate. According to Palace sources and old documents, this weapon was brought into Cambodia under the rule of King Ponhea Nou, who converted to Isla after marrying a Malaysian princess.

Following royal tradition, this young princess offered the King a Kriss that had come from her ancestors, once rulers of Malaysia.

The Kriss was made of ivory, and was considered a powerful talisman by the Khmers, and a bringer of good luck. The Kriss, like the Sacred Sword and the Victory Spear, disappeared from the Royal Palace in 1970.

• The Preah Veal Vichani

The Fan has also its origin in Angkor and can be seen in the reliefs of the ancient temple. The Fan seemed to be associated with the idea that the divine king should enjoy coolness and comfort, particularly during the hot season.

• The Betel Nut set, the Receptacle, the Water Urn and the Libation Vessel

These items of personal use were associated in the former Indochina with rank not only for the ruler but also for senior officials, who were presented with a set by the king when they received a promotion. Normally crafted in gold or silver and gold-plated, they are nowadays part of the royal regalia of the monarchies in Cambodia and Thailand.

The Cambodian Royal Regalia described above were held to be sacred and were therefore venerated by the people. Their disappearance from the Royal Palace in 1970 caused many in Cambodia to believe that there would be no peace in Cambodia until these sacred objects were found and restored to their appropriate place in the Royal Palace.

In 1993, when the Cambodian monarchy was restored and His Majesty King Norodom Sihanouk was elected monarch for the second time, His Majesty instructed that no new regalia be made for his coronation ceremony because of the difficult financial situation of his country.

King Monivong leaves the Royal Palace to visit his people on the day of his coronation— 25 July 1928.

© Collection Léon Busy, Musée Albert Kahn

THE BAKUS

THE BAKUS are the descendants of the ancient Brahman priests, who were given the privilege of conducting the worship of the royal palace by King Jayavarman II. The king granted this privilege to his Brahman chaplain, a priest known by the name of Shivakaivalya and, to his descendants.

This caste used to have several hundred families in Cambodia but was reduced just to a few during the brutal Khmers Rouges' rule. They dress and behave like all other Cambodians, the only difference being that they do not cut their hair. They practice certain abstinences not practiced by ordinary Cambodians and adhere strictly to certain traditions in their homes.

Their main task is to conduct worship in the royal palace, but they also served as guardians of the Cambodian regalia until their disappearance in 1970. The remaining Bakus are lodged in a special building of the Royal Palace.

A ROYAL CORONATION

THE ROYAL CORONATION of a Cambodian monarch can take place several days, months or even years after the election of the sovereign. In effect, the king assumes functions immediately after his election and the coronation is essentially a religious and symbolic ceremony designed to bring divine blessings upon the elected monarch.

Following the election of the new king, the court astrologers are requested to determine the most auspicious date for the coronation ceremony. In accordance with the Kram Preah Reachea Prapdaphisek (Law on the Coronation of Kings, promulgated in the second half of the 18th century) the appropriate date is chosen and the preparations for the event begin.

The Appisek (Ceremonial Bath)

Following seven days of rites and ceremonies performed by the court Bakus, during which the fire is blessed and water to be used for the ceremony purified, the sovereign is solemnly presented to the people in the Throne Hall. A special, white, bathing pavilion has been prepared in front of the Throne Hall; the sovereign takes off his ceremonial robes and exchanges them for a light white bathing robe. The chiefs of the Buddhist Order then proceed to drop the water previously purified and consecrated on the Sovereign's head. A light shower is then released from a canopy above through the petals of a golden lotus, giving celestial significance to the shower.

While the ceremonial bath is in progress the Bakus play their ceremonial music. The sovereign then dons his ceremonial robes and addresses the Buddhist monks present declaring that he is the servant and protector of Buddhism and that he will always be loyal to Buddhism.

At the end of the Buddhist ritual, the Buddhist monks withdraw to allow the Brahman ceremony to take place.

The Brahman Consecration

Three Bakus lead the sovereign to the audience hall within the Throne Hall and ask him to be seated on the elevated throne, the symbolic representation of Mount Meru. The king turns to each of the eight principal directions of the living space, each represented by a Brahman priest, and then drinks from a conch shell, washes his face with the reminder of the water and blows the shell to produce a sound like a trumpet.

The sovereign then welcomes in his arms a statue of Shiva and one of Vishnu and swears in front of the Brahman idols kept in the palace to maintain the ancient national traditions. The king then receives his kingdom: earth, waters, mountains and forests which the chief Bakus presents to him on behalf of his people. The chief Bakus then places the crown or Mokot on the sovereign's head, and the king dons the golden slippers and symbolically takes possession of the other items of his regalia by touching them.

The Brahman ritual ends with the sovereign coming down from the elevated throne and sitting on the ordinary throne, where he receives the function with sacred oil from the chief Bakus.

The Pradakshina (Circular Procession of the Nobles)

The last part of the coronation ceremony is the Pradakshina. The ladies of the court, the princes and princesses, the mandarins and nobles, each bearing a lighted candle circulate around the throne three times, keeping their right shoulder towards the sovereign. Just before the end of the ceremony the mandarins and other senior court officials place the insignia of their rank in front of the throne. The sovereign will return them the following morning thus giving the officials a new mandate to continue in their respective functions. The ceremony ends with the king travelling in a royal cortege through the principal avenues of the capital, where the people have their first contact with their new sovereign.

The consecration of the queen used to be held in private. Normally it took place only in the presence of the ladies of the court and with their assistance. After three days of chanting by Buddhist monks, on the third day the queen received the lustral water and sacred oil from the king.

KHEMARIN PALACE

J ust to the North of the Throne Hall stands the Khemarin Palace, an imposing structure in the traditional Khmer style with a green and orange tiled roof. It was built in 1931 by King Monivong, who decided to abandon the old royal residence built for King Norodom by the French Protectorate, because it would be more expensive to repair it than to build a new one.

King Monivong's father, King Sisowath, had already expressed his desire to have a new residence built. In a letter to the Résident Supérieur, on 9 March 1921, the king wrote:

"Having examined with you again the plans of our new residence, we have seen that the new layout and the lengthy space of the apartments require a delay of four or five years for the execution of the works and expenditure that seems exaggerated to me.....The apartment in which I currently reside in the Throne room has been designed for short stays of the King only, during his attendance at ceremonies; we would like, therefore, to move to more permanent quarters as soon as possible."

This caused the French authorities to request, through their diplomatic mission in Siam, some plans and photos of the palace of the king of Siam.

Another example of superb Khmer craftsmanship—an entrance to the Khemarin Palace.

On 21 September 1921, the French minister in Bangkok wrote to the French Resident Superieur in Phnom Penh as follows:

"I have the honour to send you four photographs of the palace of H.M. the King in Bangkok, but as far as the plans are concerned the Siamese government regrets being unable to provide them as it is unable to make copies of them."

Nevertheless, the Cambodian architect in charge of the construction of the Palace, Neak Okhna Tep Nimith Mak, managed to produce a sketch of the future residence which pleased King Sisowath; but plans to build a new residence were abandoned because of the monarch's declining health.

On the ascension of King Monivong to the throne, the question of a royal residence was raised again. From an architectural point of view, the king and the French authorities wanted to build a structure purely in Cambodian style. But as it was to be the king's residence, the decision was reached that it should be both representative of the king's status as well as modern enough to cater to the needs of an evolving monarchy.

The plans drawn called for a reception area, where the king could receive distinguished foreign visitors, a large dining room for state dinners, a smaller private dining room, a study for the king and separate apartments for the king and queen plus guest rooms for foreign heads of state.

The construction began on 24 June 1931 with the building company Fong Chhoun in charge of the work.

The history of the Khemarin Palace is unavoidably linked to tragic events that rocked Cambodia. After the coup d'état

(clockwise from above) Main dining room; Main reception area where the king gives private audiences to foreign heads of state staying at the Palace; Main study where joint declarations with visiting heads of state are signed.

Khemarin Palace

of 18 March 1970, the palace was basically abandoned. Later under the Lon Nol regime, it became the Museum of Modern Art and History. After the Khmers Rouges took over Cambodia in 1975, King Sihanouk was held prisoner in his own residence for three years. And following Vietnam's invasion of Cambodia, the Chief Military Officer of the Vietnamese Army stayed at the Palace for a while.

The Khemarin Palace was renovated in 1991 in anticipation of King Sihanouk's return and in 1995 the guest quarters were completely refurbished.

Some of the foreign personalities who have stayed at the Khemarin Palace include President Charles de Gaulle of France, President Josip Broz "Tito" of Yugoslavia, Emperor Haile Selassie of Ethiopia, and Presidents Soekarno and Soeharto of Indonesia.

The guest quarters at the Khemarin Palace have all modern comforts that ensure a pleasant stay for visitors to the Palace.

Villa Kantha Bopha

BUILT BY King Sihanouk in 1956, this small western-style villa, located west of the Khemarin Palace, serves to accommodate foreign guests. It was named after King Sihanouk's favourite daughter, H.R.H. Princess Kantha Bopha who died of leukemia at the age of four. Foreign guests who stayed at the villa include Prime Minister Chou Enlai and Marshal Chen Yi of the People's Republic of China.

The King's Gardens

BEHIND THE KHEMARIN Palace there are lush gardens which were totally abandoned after the coup d'état in 1970. In 1994, under the guidance of Her Majesty Queen Norodom Monineath, the gardens were restored to their former splendour, with native plants and stone sculptures of Khmer deities creating a heavenly ambience to the well-tended gardens.

Vihear Suor

THE ROYAL CHAPEL, known as Vihear Suor, is adjacent to the Khemarin Palace on the north side. It was built in 1930 during the reign of King Monivong. Vihear Suor can be translated as the "August temple of the paradise of Indra". It is a kind of small temple supported on the type of pillars very common in tropical countries, where the rainy season often causes floods.

This charming little chapel, built on the model of a temple of the same name about 20 kilometres from Phnom Penh, is used by the king and the royal family for religious ceremonies.

© Mak Remissa

Khemarin Palace

CHANCHHAYA PAVILION

The Chanchhaya Pavilion (The Moonlight Pavilion), also known as the Royal Tribune, was built in 1913/1914 to an identical plan and in the same style as the wooden building originally constructed on the instructions of King Norodom in 1866, when he transferred his residence to Phnom Penh.

The Chanchhaya Pavilion is located near the northeast corner of the wall enclosing the Palace grounds, of which it forms part, and its elegant spire dominates the esplanade gardens which stretch down to the river.

The Chanchhaya Pavilion has served successively as a training place for the Royal Ballet, to show classical dances to visiting foreign heads of state, and as a Royal Tribune, from which the Cambodian sovereign addresses the crowd assembled to show their loyalty when events of national importance take place.

In recent years it has also been used for state banquets in honour of visiting foreign heads of state such as the King of Malaysia, the President of the Philippines and the President of Indonesia.

The dances were performed in a space marked out in the centre of the floor around which the guests were seated. The singers were located to the north of this space, on the side occupied by the green room, while the musicians were placed opposite on the south side of the building. At ground level there are two rooms, the larger one reserved for the musicians while the other is occupied by the personnel of the administrative service attached to the Royal Ballet.

Costumes and jewellery used by the dancers were housed in rooms situated beneath the Throne Hall and also partly in the Palace Museum, but most were lost after the coup d'état against the then Prince Sihanouk in March 1970 and have never been recovered.

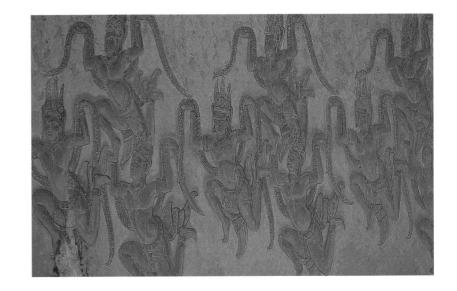

(below) A stately venue for state banquets—a dated photograph showing the interior of the Chanchhaya Pavilion. (right) Apsara dance—as seen on a wall of the Pavilion.

© Collection Albert Kahn, Musée Albert Kahn

THE ROYAL BALLET

FROM THE BEGINNING of the 14th century, the arts of music and dancing, which had held an important place in the civilisation of Angkor, declined rapidly. The preceding century had already seen the virtual disappearance of the ancient Brahman cult which in turn had dispersed the sacred dancers attached to the numerous Shivaistic and Vishnuistic temples, increasingly deserted as the years went by. Some were able to join the troupe of royal dancers, but most had no alternative but to return to their native villages far from the royal capital.

Dancing itself played no part in the newly adopted, much simpler ceremonies of Theravada Buddhism, and soon it became incorporated into the pre-Brahman popular rites, which are still performed and were thus enriched by this new influence. Dancing played a leading role in the popularisation of the Ramayana and other ancient legends still being portrayed in the villages, which helped preserve the art of these sacred dancers after more than 500 years.

The fall of Angkor in 1431 and the subsequent frequent moves of the royal capital, which was continually threatened by Siamese and Vietnamese invasions, proved fatal to the maintenance or even the partial reconstitution of a group of court musicians and dancers. There are no records or photos surviving from this tragic period, and even the Spanish, Portuguese and Dutch travellers of the sixteenth, seventeenth and eighteenth centuries did not mention or overlooked the very existence of the palace dancers in their written and oral accounts of their trips.

Accordingly, we shall never know what became of the Royal Ballet in the four centuries between the fall of Angkor and the rebirth of the Khmer monarchy with King Ang Duong in 1841. And yet classical dancing, even in the style performed today, has preserved the Angkorean traditions.

This is clear from the stone portrayals of dancers in the great temples of the ninth to thirteenth centuries. However, the court orchestras with their harps, trumpets and large gongs, as depicted in the Bayon temple carvings, seem to have completely disappeared from the people's lives and

A royal dancer poses in front of the Throne Hall.

memories. Angkorean music was thus lost, and it has not been possible to detect what part it may have contributed to today's ballet music.

We should not be surprised by this gradual separation of two forms of art—music and dancing—which we might have imagined to be closely linked. In the Cambodian ballet tradition the music follows and supports the dancers, rather than guiding them as in other styles of dancing. The orchestra is there to mark the rhythm and stress different passages, and its composition therefore does not follow any fixed rules.

Today's classical dances are unlike the superb displays of Angkorean times, as in the intervening centuries successive Khmer sovereigns were compelled to pledge the whole of the royal treasure, including the tiaras and gold jewellery of the Royal Ballet, to levy armies or to pay for the departure of foreign armies.

The rebirth of Cambodian classical dances in the nineteenth century owes a lot to Siam, which had been the cause of their decline a few centuries earlier. It was at the court of the king of Siam, where traditional Khmer dances had been preserved unbroken, that Cambodian princes and princesses rediscovered the whole system of music and dancing handed down from the sovereigns of Angkor, and brought it back with them to Cambodia.

To explain why the Siamese adopted the Khmers' art forms, it is necessary to go back in history. When the first T'ais of the southern provinces of China began slowly emigrating towards the Mekong basin, they came into contact with the Angkorean Khmers and adopted their customs, beliefs, art forms and technology.

The first kings of Siam adopted the Angkorean administrative and political structure, which was far superior to their own, and used them to build up their own state organisation. T'ai princes, who were called upon to rule over ever larger and richer lands, were at pains to imitate as carefully as possible the court of Angkor, whose splendour shone over the whole of Southern Asia.

Therefore music and dancing, which held such an important place in rituals and festivals, were among the first innovations to be introduced at the courts of Sukhothai and, later on, Ayutthaya.

The classical art of choreography, which has flourished at the Siamese court until today, certainly came under T'ai, Mon and Burmese influence, but has, nevertheless, remained in essence Khmer. The Siamese, like most Asian peoples, have attached great importance to the preservation of living art forms in their original state, handed down to them by history for safe keeping.

A drawing from a Dutch magazine showing the Royal Ballet performing for foreign guests.

The Royal Palace of Phnom Penh

The Revival of the Royal Ballet

King Ang Duong (1841-1859), who came to the Cambodian throne in 1841, was an enlightened sovereign, a protector of the arts and personally highly skilled in traditional poetry. He was the author of short stories as well as a number of songs and verbal accompaniments to classical dancing.

When Ang Duong became king, he found that classical dancing was on the verge of total disappearance. The few dancers that remained at the court still preserved the classical tradition but had introduced some rather unorthodox quick shoulder and chest movements, and a way of shaking the body. Men also took part in the dancing, or at least made the few customary movements of hands and feet which accompanied the popular alternating songs known as "ayay". They imitated Vietnamese opera movements with their legs bent and very slightly apart and their elbows thrown back at shoulder height.

Ang Duong therefore undertook to return to the royal dances their original meaning and classical beauty, as well as to restore them to their level of dignity in the votive ceremonies to the gods and the solemn palace festivals. This renewal and reorganisation was carried out with the utmost care, and most of the changes introduced at that time have remained until today.

After reforming and establishing the choreographic side of the ballet, the King turned his attention to the costumes. Until then, the dancers had worn the Angkorean costume, almost unchanged from that of the stone figures in the great temples. It consisted mainly of a light Sampot, often draped round the waist and leaving leg movements completely free.

The reforms undertaken by Ang Duong demanded heavy pieces of silver and gold-braided silk, either because the semi-nudity of the dancers was no longer suited to the morals and beliefs of the time, or more probably in imitation of the Siamese. This new addition completely changed the appearance of the dancers and, by greatly limiting their freedom of movement, was to have a considerable effect on the future of Khmer choreography.

King Ang Duong took great care in designing costumes for each of the legendary characters portrayed by the ballet. The jackets and bodices, the embroidered scarves, the tiaras, the jewels, all belonging to princes and princesses of different rank, the green or red Sampots and the warriors' tunics with magic emblems were carefully studied and fixed once and for all in their shape, colour and design. They have not changed since then.

When King Norodom assumed the throne in 1860, classical dance had recovered some of its ancient prestige, and it soon became a great honour for court officials, ministers and senior dignitaries to have their children admitted to the palace's school of dancing.

When France established its protectorate in Cambodia in 1863, this caused certain changes in court life. Firstly, the original troupe of 500 dancers was gradually reduced to about 100 dancers by 1904 and the royal dancing troupe itself was disbanded.

The children of government and palace dignitaries were sent to Western-style schools to study or simply drawn into the royal entourage depending on their age. Some of the dancers who left the palace formed their own private dancing troupes, which were promptly taken under the protection and financial support of ministers and senior court officials to be presented to the king on special occasions.

King Norodom himself admired music, and studied it more than dancing. Initially he was particularly fond of the music in the Pinpeat style, which flourished after his ascension to the throne. But later the king turned his attention to ancient music forms, particularly to music accompanied by the Chrieng Chapei guitar.

In 1872, the king went on a visit to Hong Kong, Manila and Singapore. In the Philippines the king was greatly impressed by the music skills of the Filipinos and decided to take some musicians back to Cambodia to teach modern music. The musicians were well received, and in due course also influenced Cambodian classical dancing. Special quarters were built for the Filipinos beside the current Royal Palace, facing the National Museum, which promptly became known by the locals as "Villa Manila".

The famous "coconut dance", often rendered by the Royal Ballet, is one of the dances from the Philippines adopted by Cambodia.

The rehearsals of what was to become the royal orchestra were held at the Palace, which also welcomed Chinese musicians, who were allowed to teach their art to ladies of the court.

While in Singapore, King Norodom was impressed by the skills of Malay coachmen, and soon afterwards some of them were invited to Cambodia to live under the protection of the Royal Palace. This small group of immigrants took an interest in Khmer music and dancing, and with royal approval began participating in the activities of the royal troupe, thus bringing further external influences to the dancing. Later on, the daughter of one of the Malay coachmen was to become a star performer in the Royal Ballet.

King Norodom's generosity began drawing artists from many nationalities to Cambodia and they were always given a warm welcome at the Royal Palace and court. Most of them had a deep interest in the Royal Ballet and thus were given every opportunity to learn Khmer music and dancing, as well as to cultivate their own art and participate in the preparation of small spectacles for the king. In this way, Burmese and Laotian choreographic influences also began to appear in Khmer dancing.

In 1903, the Royal Ballet reached its peak with the first-ever performance of the Ramayana, on the occasion of the consecration of the Wat Preah Keo Morokat.

According to a well-established court custom, the dancers could, if they wished, leave the Royal Ballet for good when the monarch passed away. Thus on the death of King Norodom in 1904, more than two thirds of the dancers left the Palace, *"too distressed"*, it is said, *"by the absence of the old monarch, who used to watch the rehearsals every day, to have the courage to continue their dancing"*. Only the younger dancers seem to have remained.

King Norodom was succeeded by King Sisowath in 1904. Sisowath shared the same interest in the Royal Ballet as his father, King Ang Duong, and took steps to prevent its disappearance. He enlisted the help of Prince

Scene of classical Khmer dance in front of Angkor Wat.

Sutharot's mother, who had once been first dancer of the Royal Ballet in the role of a princess and had subsequently been given the name of Khun Chom Bosseba, (Bosseba being the legendary princess whom she had incarnated, it is said, with unequal perfection). Khun Chom Bosseba devoted two years to the training and classical formation of the dancers, remaining faithful to the principles she had herself received from King Ang Duong.

When King Sisowath visited France in 1906 he took with him the Royal Ballet, consisting at the time of 42 dancers, 8 rhythm keepers, 12 musicians, a choir of 12 as well as some jewellers who helped with the costumes. The troupe was then directed by the sovereign's eldest daughter Princess Sounpady. The performances of the Royal Ballet in Marseilles and Paris were described as triumphant.

After its return to Cambodia, the Royal Ballet again fell into a period of decline. By 1911, King Sisowath allowed the dancers to leave the troupe whenever they wished, and he encouraged young dancers to attend school instead of taking their dancing lessons.

In 1922 a small group of dancers was taken on another trip to France, but after this brief revival classical dancing seemed to sink even further into oblivion. The king had reached his 86th year, was ill and almost blind. He no longer had the strength or the financial means to struggle against the loss of traditions and the Western influences reaching Cambodia.

The Royal Ballet's collapse was imminent and French scholars, began speaking out to save it. George Groslier, an eminent scholar on Khmer art wrote:

"We are witnessing the agony of Khmer dancers. They are no more than shadows. They are down to their last costumes. The Princesses are selling or pawning their jewellery. Sculptors are harder to find; the royal painters want to learn perspective and oil painting, and the women by their huts in the shade of the banana trees no longer weave the beautiful sampots of years ago."

In the last years of King Sisowath's reign, the French Protectorate authorities began to take a direct interest in the Royal Ballet, and George Groslier, by then Art Director of the Protectorate, was called on to help revive daily rehearsals of the ballet and to study ways of restoring classical dancing to its former prestige.

In 1928 King Monivong (1927-1941) was crowned, and the French authorities and the Royal Palace administration reached an agreement, later approved by the monarch, for a group of dancers to be placed under the guidance of the School of Fine Arts. This was a complete break with tradition, but it was accepted because it was a way of saving the ballet from extinction. However, the experiment did not last.

In effect, the dancers who had dedicated themselves to the sacred art, in the tradition of Angkor, suddenly found themselves working as civil servants. However, the troupe made some technical progress which allowed them to participate successfully at the Saigon Exhibition of 1928.

The trip to Saigon had unforeseen and dramatic consequences. The chief guardian of the dancers' jewellery seized a small treasure, including 25 kilogrammes of gold and several more of gilded silver which had been entrusted to him by the king, and fled to Thailand. The Royal Palace was shocked by the event and decided to take immediate control of the dancers, musicians, dressers and administrative staff of the Royal Ballet.

It was not easy to return to the traditional organisation of the Royal Ballet. As civil servants, the dancers had been given freedom to lead a private life, and many had married. Thus, when recalled to the Royal Palace, they were unable to reconcile the old tradition with their altered status, and once again the Royal Ballet was reduced to a troupe of about 12 dancers and roughly the same number of choristers, rhythm keepers and dressers, less than the strict number required for religious or ceremonial dances performed during offerings to the gods or the Sovereign's birthday.

The Royal Palace decided to call former members of the Royal Ballet, now running their own private dancing troupes, to return to the palace to make up its depleted ranks.

In 1931 the French government issued an invitation to the Royal Ballet to travel to Paris, but because of the problems mentioned above, the Royal Palace turned down the invitation. At about the same time, a former royal dancer named Soy Sangvann, married to King Sisowath's youngest son Prince Vong Kath, formed her own classical dancing troupe and succeeded in getting the French government to invite her troupe to Paris, where they achieved the same reputation the Royal Ballet had received back in 1906.

On their return to Cambodia, Soy Sangvann's company was given official recognition by the French authorities and began receiving a subsidy from them on condition that the troupe performed for eminent guests of the Résident Supérieur and even at the Angkor temple. It did not, however, receive the title of Royal Ballet, which was kept by the few dancers remaining from the original Royal Palace troupe, who continue to perform at ritual ceremonies.

Observers at the time felt that this was the end of the Royal Ballet, as the palace troupe was forgotten and the new private troupes drifted towards Western dancing forms. But it seems that classical dancing refused to die and was kept alive in people's memories until another revival could take place.

It was at this dismal time for the royal troupe that another former star dancer of the Royal Ballet during the reign of King Sisowath, Khun Meak, began teaching a group of about twenty very young girls. Khun Meak had been saddened by the decadence of the Royal Ballet, and after four years of training in the most traditional techniques of Khmer dancing, the troupe of girls had acquired a solid basis and showed tremendous promise.

Khun Meak then transferred the troupe to Princess Kossomak, daughter of King Monivong, who placed them under her patronage and devoted herself to the task of completing the troupe's training.

But Princess Kossomak's activities for the Royal Ballet were interrupted by the second world war, which for Cambodia meant the Siamese aggression of 1940 and the loss of the province of Battambang and important parts of Siemreap and Kompong Thom. King Monivong, deeply saddened by these events, died in 1941.

Classical Khmer dancers on the landing at Sras Srang.

The Royal Ballet under the Reign of King Sihanouk

King Norodom Sihanouk (1941-1955) succeeded King Monivong in 1941 at the young age of nineteen. The Protectorate authorities who had chosen King Sihanouk because he was, in their view, the most "manageable" among the Khmer princes who could be king, took advantage of the king's young age to transfer the administration of the Royal Palace to the Cambodian government, which was under the control of the French authorities.

This new arrangement almost finished the Royal Ballet, and matters were not helped by the Résident Supérieur, who was ignorant of Khmer customs and traditions and not really interested in the arts, and informed

The late Princess Norodom Sujata (left), daughter of King Sihanouk in a scene from a classical Cambodian dance.

Princess Kossamak that the Royal Ballet must be sacrificed in the new drive for economic austerity. The Résident Supérieur also felt that Soy Sangvann's private troupe could be used when a classical dance troupe was required for Palace ceremonies.

Princess Kossomak strongly objected to this arrangement proposed by the French authorities but she was unable to change the Résident Supérieur's mind, bent on saving 600 riels a month for the upkeep of the Royal Ballet.

With the support of her son, the newly crowned King, Princess Kossomak decided that it was necessary at all costs to preserve the Royal Ballet. King Sihanouk supplied a monthly allowance from his own limited resources and the Royal Palace authorities were instructed to provide lodgings for the royal dancers, some of whom had served under two or even three Kings. As soon as the six months of official mourning for King Monivong were over, training of the Royal Ballet began again as had been done in the past.

Princess Kossomak also managed to gather all the former teachers of the Royal Ballet, who returned to the Royal Palace to help in the training of new recruits. They had all been first dancers of the Royal Ballet under previous kings, and each was an expert in one particular role of the many presented by the royal troupe.

Princess Kossomak thus became not only the protector of the Royal Ballet but also a kind of director, playing a leading role in the training and changes undertaken by the troupe. A new choreography, a new order of events were drawn up for classical dances and the costumes were completely restored. The Royal Ballet was able to put a wonderful performance on the occasion of the state visit to Cambodia of Emperor Bao Dai of Annam (Vietnam) in 1942.

But apparently the French authorities were still unhappy with the reborn Royal Ballet, and they again expressed their disapproval of the programme and suggested the troupe should be replaced by the private troupe of Soy Sangvann. King Sihanouk decided that it was time to use his royal power to protect the Royal Ballet, and after a dinner on the occasion of his birthday, he presented to his guests the new programme of the new Royal Ballet, which won the emphatic admiration of all those present, including the French authorities.

In this way, the Royal Ballet once again became the sole Depository of Khmer classical dancing traditions, and in 1962 the Royal

Ballet was given an administrative statute, similar to that possessed by national ballet ensembles in Europe, such as the Royal Ballet of the United Kingdom.

The statute made clear provisions for every administrative contingency. In 1962, staff of the Royal Ballet numbered 254, with 2 professors, 17 dancing mistresses, one principal dancer, 5 first dancers, 25 dancers, 160 students, 14 dressers and make-up women, 4 dressmakers and 6 apprentices, 6 custodians of the jewellery, 10 singers, 4 buffoons, 24 musicians and 4 music students.

Princess Kossomak became Queen Kossomak Nearireath on the abdication of King Norodom Sihanouk in 1955, and she ensured that the Royal Ballet became one of Cambodia's most loved and respected institutions.

The Royal Ballet made several trips abroad and was always welcomed as a splendid ambassador for Cambodia.

After the coup d'état by General Lon Nol in March 1970, the Royal Ballet suffered another blow as the monarchy was abolished and with the ancient institution all things related to it. The Royal Ballet went through a period of turmoil, as different military officers tried to lure dancers into private troupes formed by their wives or concubines.

The Royal Ballet's jewellery disappeared and staff were dispersed. The Royal Palace itself became a museum and Queen Kossomak Nearireath was held under house arrest. The republicans were not interested in the ancient traditions of the kings of Angkor.

The republicans did not last long. In 1975 they were overthrown by the Khmers Rouges, who established a Marxist state where royal dancing had no place. Many dancers from what was left of the royal troupe died under terrible conditions, and the few survivors went into hiding until the Vietnamese army drove the Khmers Rouges away.

The People's Republic of Kampuchea kept the Royal Palace as a Museum and the survivors of the Royal Ballet were given space at the Tonle Bassac Theatre to rehearse and train new recruits.

Later on, responsibility for the dancing troupe was transferred to the School of Fine Arts. The troupe was allowed to make a trip abroad in the late 1980s, but the trip ended with the disappearance of some dancers who asked for political asylum in the United States. Further trips were immediately halted and the dancers were considered untrustworthy by the government.

Following the Paris Peace Agreements of October 1991, King Sihanouk and other members of the Royal Cambodian Family returned to Cambodia from exile abroad. Princess Buppha Devi, a daughter of King Sihanouk, who had become renowned during the late 1960s as principal dancer of the Royal Ballet, was appointed Vice Minister of Culture and given responsibility for strengthening a new dance troupe that soon afterwards became the Royal Cambodian Ballet.

With the restoration of the monarchy in Cambodia in September 1993, the Royal Ballet regained its previous position as a "national treasure", and the graceful dancers continue to provide joy as well as hope to a great and ancient people still troubled by the trauma resulting from many years of civil warfare.

Princess Buppha Devi (left), herself a star of the Royal Ballet in the 60s, played a key role in restoring the ancient art.

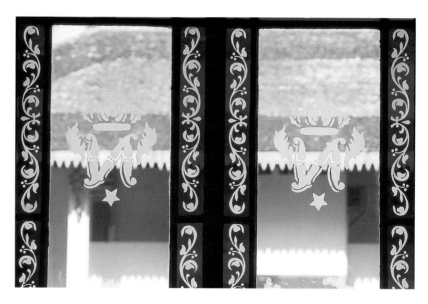

NAPOLEON PAVILION

Also known as the "Suez Pavilion", this little palace is an all-metal structure built of forged iron for Empress Eugénie of France, wife of Emperor Napoléon III, in 1869 in Ismailia, Egypt, on the occasion of the inauguration of the Suez Canal.

It was later presented, by Emperor Napoléon III to King Norodom of Cambodia in 1876. There was no need even to change the badges bearing the royal letter "N" as the initial was the same for both sovereigns.

The insignia of Emperor Napoléon III engraved in the glass panes also serves as insignia for King Norodom. (This photograph was taken inside the building.)

When the structure arrived in Phnom Penh in 1876, it was the first permanent building of the Royal Palace. Much taken with its modern style, King Norodom decided to make it his personal residence, but there is no record that the sovereign ever lived there.

In 1991, following the Paris Agreements on Cambodia and the return of King Norodom Sihanouk to Cambodia, the French government funded a complete refurbishing of the Pavilion.

Today the Pavilion has been transformed into a small museum, where memorabilia belonging to the Cambodian Royal Family are exhibited.

(above) Stained glasses and (bottom) a bronze staircase are among the many features of the Napoleon Pavilion with distinct Western influence.

A collection of portraits of past Cambodian monarchs are among other memorabilia on display in the Napoleon Pavilion.

Napoleon Pavilion

OTHER BUILDINGS

RUNG DAM REI HALL

Rung Dam Rei Hall or the Elephant's Hall was built in 1892 in the southern part of Wat Preah Keo Morokat. Elephants were the main means of transport of Cambodian kings from the Angkor era and they were also used when the capital moved first to Oudong and then to Phnom Penh. Cambodian kings set on elephants for transport from one place to another, for hunting and to lead their armies into battle against foreign invaders. Elephants were the advanced convoy, indicating great power so as to intimidate the enemy. This is shown clearly in the bas-reliefs of Angkor Wat, the Bayon Temples and the so-called Elephant Terrace of Angkor Wat.

Elephants also played an important role in transporting stone blocks for the construction of the complex of temples and monuments at Angkor.

For the Cambodians, elephants symbolised happiness and they were said to subdue all evil spirits. Their ivory tusks were valuable items of decoration in the houses of the Cambodian nobility. They also symbolised prosperity.

For instance, on the occasion of the ceremony invoking the god who sent the rain, the elephants were ordered to suck water into their trunks and spray it everywhere in the form of rainfall. This is why successive Cambodian sovereigns employed a group of elephant-keepers and trainers to take care of them and keep them ready for transport during ceremonies and battle duties.

Today, the elephants are gone from the compound and the Hall has been transformed and renovated as a museum under the royal guidance and patronage of Her Majesty Queen Norodom Monineath Sihanouk.

The Museum displays antiques and reproduction artifacts and paraphernalia used for different royal ceremonies in the past, such as the royal coronation procession, royal funeral rites and other religious rituals.

The main aim of the Museum is to show the different ceremonies that took place and in which elephant armies were used, during the reign of King Norodom (1860-1904).

The elegant Rung Dam Rei Hall now serves as a museum where a vast array of equipment used for royal ceremonies is on display.

PHOCHANI PAVILION

BUILT INITIALLY as a venue for the performance of the Royal Ballet in 1912, this has since been used to hold royal audiences given by the sovereign to the people and also to host dance and theatre performances for distinguished foreign visitors.

The Hall is built in the traditional Khmer style as an entirely open pavilion without any windows. Performances normally take place in the evening, and the evening breeze cools the audience down.

SAHAMETREI PAVILION

THE SAHAMETREI PAVILION was built in 1950 and was the private residence of the late Queen Kossomak Nearireath, mother of the current sovereign, where she moved to live after the death of her beloved husband King Norodom Suramarit in 1960. The Queen remained in this pavilion after the coup d'état of 18 March 1970 and only left it when she left Cambodia for China in 1973.

The Sahametrei Pavilion remained unused for many years, until 1991 when staff of His Majesty King Norodom Sihanouk moved there after the monarch's return to Cambodia from exile in China. It then became the Secretariat of the Supreme National Council of Cambodia from 1991 to 1993. Renovated in 1994, it is now used as accommodation for senior staff of visiting foreign heads of state who are official guests of Their Majesties the King and Queen.

© Mak Remissa

© Dominic Faulder

DAMNAK CHAN

BUILT IN 1956, during the reign of King Norodom Suramarit to house the High Council of the Throne, this building has a roof in traditional Khmer style while the main structure is in Western style, allowing officials to work in the premises.

The building previously had an office for King Sihanouk, and served as the Ministry of Culture in the late 1970s and 1980s.

It was also used for meetings of the Supreme National Council of Cambodia from 1991 to 1993 and since then it has become the office of the Minister of the Royal Palace. All the administrative services of the Royal Palace are located in this building.

Photo courtesy: H.M. the King

ROYAL INSTITUTIONS

THE MONARCHY

The present dynasty can be traced back to the Angkor empire, which included parts of Thailand, Laos, Vietnam and all of present-day Cambodia, at its peak between the 9th and 14th centuries. Gradually Cambodia's political and economic centre moved from Angkor to Phnom Penh, and by the 18th century Thailand and Vietnam were vying for political control of the country. Cambodia was dominated by its neighbours, until France turned it into a protectorate in 1864. South Cambodia became South Vietnam when France gave it to Vietnam, and France granted full independence to Cambodia on 9 November 1953 following a royal crusade led by His Majesty King Norodom Sihanouk.

In 1955, King Norodom Sihanouk abdicated the throne to enter politics. As elected Head of State, he was successful in keeping Cambodia neutral and free from the escalating war ravaging Vietnam and Laos, but he was ousted in March 1970 by pro-USA members of his government. King Sihanouk, who was at the time visiting Moscow, travelled to Beijing where he launched an appeal to all Cambodian patriotic forces to join him in fighting the Americans and the Lon Nol regime in Phnom Penh. One of the first groups to answer Sihanouk's appeal was the Khmers Rouges, a radical communist guerrilla movement.

H.M. King Norodom Sihanouk taken for a walk to meet his people on the day of his coronation in 1941.

Chronology of Cambodian Kings

The following chronology of Cambodian kings has been compiled from different sources, mostly works by French scholars and explorers, which are duly acknowledged in the bibliography of this book.

From the end of the Mahidharapura period the record of subsequent Cambodian kings becomes rather confused and the documents available give contradictory accounts of the reigns of some of them, while the dates of their rule do not appear to be accurate. It is known that Angkor ceased to be the capital in 1431 following a Siamese invasion. This period of the Cambodian monarchy was marked by the interference of Cambodia's two close neighbours, Siam and Annam, in the selection and appointment of monarchs and by conflict among the Cambodian rulers themselves.

The author of this book has reconstructed this period as best as he could from the little information available, but he is unable to give precise dates of the rule of the monarchs that followed the fall of Angkor:

Fu-Nan Period

Kaundinya	c. 400-420
Jayavarman	c. 480-514
Rudravarman	c. 514-539

Chen-La Period

Bhavavarman I	c. 550-N.A.
Sitrasena	c. 600-616
Isanavarman I	c. 616-635
Bhavavarman II	c. 635-656
Jayavarman I	c. 657-681
Jayadevi	c. 713-N.A.
Jayavarman II	c. 770-834
Jayavarman III	c. 834-870
Indravarman	c. 877-889 (Builder of the Temples of Pra Koh and Bakong.

Angkor Period

Yashovarman I	c. 889-910 (Establishment of Yashodharapura or Angkor as capital.)
Harshavarman I	c. 911-923
Isanavarman II	c. 923-928
Jayavarman IV	c. 928-941
Harshavarman II	c. 942-944
Rajendravarman II	c. 944-968
Jayavarman V	c. 968-1001
Udayadityavarman I	c. 1001-1002
Jayaviravarman	c. 1002-1010
Suryavarman I	c. 1011-1050
Udayadityavarman II	c. 1050-1066 (Builder of Baphuon Temple.)
Harshavarman III	c. 1066-1080

Mahidharapura Period

Jayavarman VI	c. 1080-1107 (Builder of Phimai.)
Dharanindravarman	c. 1107-1113
Suryavarman II	c. 1113-1150 (Builder of Angkor Wat.)
Dharanindravarman II	c. 1150-1160
Yashovarman II	c. 1160-1166
Tribhuvanadityavarman	c. 1166-1181
Jayavarman VII	c. 1181-1219 (Builder of Angkor Thom.)
Indravarman II	c. 1219-1243
Jayavarman VIII	c. 1243-1295
Indravarman III	c. 1295-1308
Srey Soryopor	N.A.
Chey Chettah II	N.A.
The Regent Outey	N.A.
Ponhea To	N.A.
Ponhea Nou	N.A.
Ang Nou	N.A.
Ang Non I	N.A.
Chan	N.A.
Batom Reachea	c. 1660-1672
Chey Chettah III	c. 1672-1673
Ang Chei	c. 1673-1674
Chey Chettah IV	c. 1675-1691
Outey	c. 1691-1695
Ang Em	c. 1699-1701
Thommo Reachea II	c. 1702-1703
Thommo Reachea II (2nd rule)	c. 1706-1710
Ang Em (2nd rule)	c. 1710-1722
Satha II	c. 1722-1736
Thommo Reachea II (3rd rule)	c. 1736-1747
Thommo Reachea III	c. 1747
Ang Thong	c. 1747-1749

Chey Chettah V	c. 1749-1755
Ang Tong	c. 1755-1758
Outey II	c. 1758-1775
Ang Non III	c. 1779
Ang Eng	c. 1779-1796
Ang Chang	c. 1796-1834
Queen Ang Mey	c. 1835-1841 (Only female ruler appearing in records, never crowned.)
Truong-Minh Giang	c. 1841-1847 (Foreign ruler.)

French Protectorate

Ang Duong	c. 1841-1859 (Unified Kingdom and reformed administration.)
Norodom (Ang Voddey)	c. 1860-1904 (Established capital in Phnom Penh and began construction of Royal Palace.)
Sisowath (Ang Sar)	c. 1904-1927
Monivong	c. 1927-1941
Norodom Sihanouk (1st rule)	c. 1941-1955 (Obtained independence from France.)

Post-colonial Period

Norodom Suramarit	c. 1955-1960 (The Cambodian monarchy was abolished on 9 October 1970 after the coup d'état and restored in 1993 after UN-supervised elections.)
Norodom Sihanouk (2nd rule)	c. 1993-

On 17 April 1975, the Khmers Rouges captured Phnom Penh and began setting up a radical agrarian society under which more than one million people died of hunger, disease, overwork and the systematic violence of the regime. In late 1978, following several attacks across the Vietnamese border, Vietnam invaded Cambodia and set up a government in Phnom Penh headed by Khmer Rouge defectors and pro-Vietnamese communists. Vietnam occupied Cambodia for almost 14 years but was forced to withdraw its forces by a concerted guerrilla campaign led by a coalition of the two non-communist resistance groups and the Khmers Rouges.

In October 1991, in Paris, a Peace Agreement was signed by the warring Cambodian factions and their respective sponsors and supporters. The country was placed under a United Nations Transitional Authority which organised elections in May 1993 from which a National Assembly and a new government were born. On 24 September 1993, a new Constitution was proclaimed which restored the country as a non-hereditary constitutional monarchy. His Majesty King Norodom Sihanouk was appointed King of Cambodia.

**(above) King Sisowath who reigned from 1904-1927.
(right) King Norodom Suramarit and Queen Kossomak Nearireath during the Coronation ceremony.**

THE KING

In the past, the kingdom of Cambodia was an absolute monarchy tempered only by the strength of its customs and traditions as well as by the religious institutions which from the nation's beginnings until today have had a powerful influence on its inhabitants.

In earlier days, "the State was the King", who enjoyed unlimited power and was considered the absolute head of the country, the army, the administration and all its institutions. The king appointed or revoked all dignitaries in the administration, established and distributed taxes and disposed at will of the country's resources.

Considered also as Supreme Judge, the king decided on who should die and who should live. He could grant amnesty or condemn to death, he could order the revision of a judgment, and any of his subjects who felt they had been denied justice could appeal to the sovereign for redress by observing certain traditional formalities—that is, by beating a drum placed in the Royal Palace or by prostrating himself in front of the monarch when the latter passed by, with his request held high over his head.

The people were deeply and sincerely attached to their hereditary chiefs, and this remains true today, particularly in the rural areas. The Khmer race has always believed that its own existence was linked to that of the sovereign.

The monarch was considered to be the living incarnation, the supreme personification of the nation and its sacred representative, who was above the law. His powers knew no boundaries, apart from those the monarch's own conscience imposed upon him in accordance with the ancient traditions and customs of royalty.

Only religion, which was well rooted among the people, escaped the authority of the sovereign, who considered it a great honour to be the natural protector of Buddhism.

Today, Cambodia's monarchy is no longer hereditary. Kings are chosen by the Council of the Throne composed of the Presidents of the Senate and the National Assembly, the Prime Minister, the two Head Monks of the Buddhist Orders of Mohanikay and Thammayut, the First and Second Vice-Presidents of the Senate and the First and Second Vice-Presidents of the National Assembly.

Cambodia being a constitutional monarchy, the functions, actions and activities of the sovereign are organised in accordance with the role the constitution has given him. The king reigns but does not rule.

The Royal Palace of Phnom Penh

THE ROYAL FAMILY

The Cambodian royal family consists of the princes and princesses, sons and grandsons, daughters and granddaughters (known in the Khmer language as "Preah Ang Mechas" and "Neac Ang Mechas" respectively) of a deceased monarch or of the reigning monarch. In the past, they enjoyed certain rights and privileges fixed both by tradition and by a Royal Decree of 1 January 1907 signed by King Sisowath.

That decree was specific in stating that the princesses could only marry princes of their rank and that marriages must be approved by the reigning monarch. The same decree also fixed the procedure that members of the royal family had to follow if they desired to renounce their rank and marry a commoner.

The decree of 1907 also allowed for disciplinary sanctions to be imposed by the monarch if any prince or princess was found to have behaved badly or had tainted royal dignity.

THE COUNCIL OF THE ROYAL FAMILY

A Royal Decree dated 12 April 1915, signed by King Sisowath, established the Council of the Royal Family which was composed of eight princes or princesses appointed by the king. The Council had supervisory and disciplinary functions.

The Council could undertake the investigation of the behaviour or activities of a particular member of the royal family and proceed to propose to the sovereign an appropriate punishment or exoneration.

The Council also provided advise to members of the royal family on various issues such as the allocation of funds from the Civil List to members of the royal family.

(left) A royal princess, daughter of King Ang Duong.
(right) One of King Ang Duong's royal consorts with her ladies-in-waiting.
(opposite page) Prince Sisowath, elder son of King Ang Duong and half-brother of King Norodom, who later became King Sisowath.

© Mak Remissa

THE CAMBODIAN MONARCHY TODAY

Today's royal institution has become more adapted to the constitutional character of the monarchy. Gone is the Civil List for all members of the royal family, who can now be found working in politics, the administration, diplomacy, the army, the arts and the economic sector.

The Cambodian monarchy remains closely linked to the small citizenry of the country, particularly to those living in the rural areas. Much of the royal budget, appropriated each year by the National Assembly, goes to help the most destitute members of Cambodian society, through a special assistance team known as "Samdech Euv's Team" (or "The King-Father's Team") personally organised and directed by His Majesty the King and ably assisted by Her Majesty Queen Norodom Monineath Sihanouk.

(above) Recent photograph of His Majesty King Norodom Sihanouk and Her Majesty Queen Norodom Monineath Sihanouk.

Genealogy of the Royal Family of Cambodia

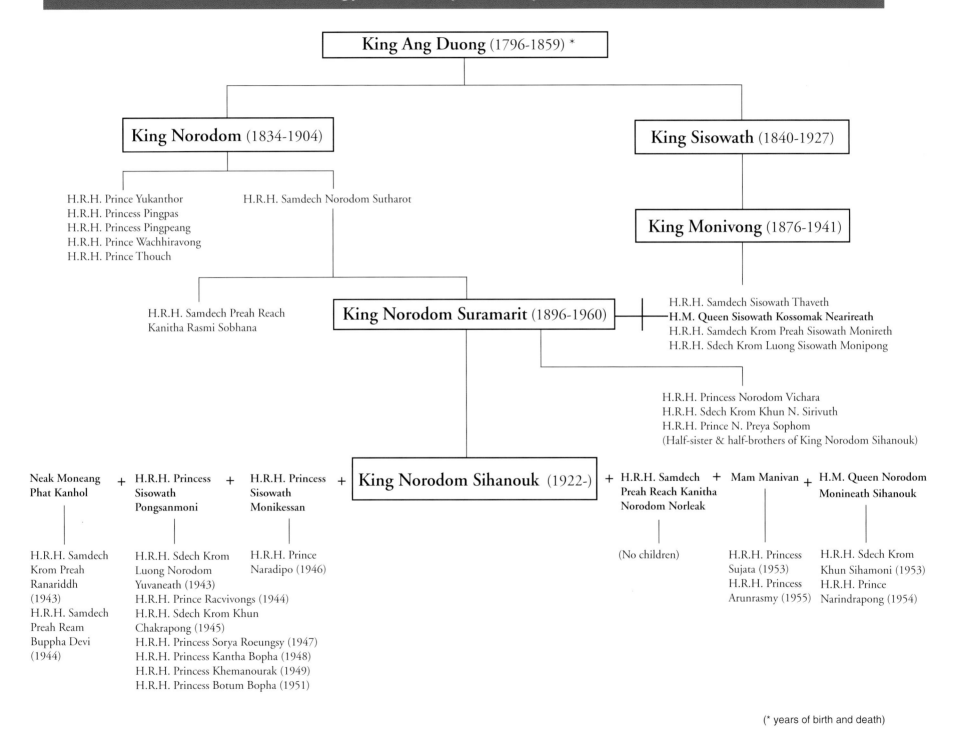

King Ang Duong (1796-1859) *

King Norodom (1834-1904)

King Sisowath (1840-1927)

H.R.H. Prince Yukanthor
H.R.H. Princess Pingpas
H.R.H. Princess Pingpeang
H.R.H. Prince Wachhiravong
H.R.H. Prince Thouch

H.R.H. Samdech Norodom Sutharot

King Monivong (1876-1941)

H.R.H. Samdech Preah Reach
Kanitha Rasmi Sobhana

King Norodom Suramarit (1896-1960)

H.R.H. Samdech Sisowath Thaveth
H.M. Queen Sisowath Kossomak Nearireath
H.R.H. Samdech Krom Preah Sisowath Monireth
H.R.H. Sdech Krom Luong Sisowath Monipong

H.R.H. Princess Norodom Vichara
H.R.H. Sdech Krom Khun N. Sirivuth
H.R.H. Prince N. Preya Sophom
(Half-sister & half-brothers of King Norodom Sihanouk)

Neak Moneang
Phat Kanhol
+ H.R.H. Princess
Sisowath
Pongsanmoni
+ H.R.H. Princess
Sisowath
Monikessan
+ King Norodom Sihanouk (1922-) + H.R.H. Samdech
Preah Reach Kanitha
Norodom Norleak
+ Mam Manivan + H.M. Queen Norodom
Monineath Sihanouk

H.R.H. Samdech
Krom Preah
Ranariddh
(1943)
H.R.H. Samdech
Preah Ream
Buppha Devi
(1944)

H.R.H. Sdech Krom
Luong Norodom
Yuvaneath (1943)
H.R.H. Prince Racvivongs (1944)
H.R.H. Sdech Krom Khun
Chakrapong (1945)
H.R.H. Princess Sorya Roeungsy (1947)
H.R.H. Princess Kantha Bopha (1948)
H.R.H. Princess Khemanourak (1949)
H.R.H. Princess Botum Bopha (1951)

H.R.H. Prince
Naradipo (1946)

(No children)

H.R.H. Princess
Sujata (1953)
H.R.H. Princess
Arunrasmy (1955)

H.R.H. Sdech Krom
Khun Sihamoni (1953)
H.R.H. Prince
Narindrapong (1954)

(* years of birth and death)

The Royal Orders of Cambodia

The Royal Order of Cambodia

This is the most senior royal decoration established in 1864 by King Norodom. It is awarded for eminent services to the Kingdom and is given in five classes: Grand Cross, Grand Officer, Commander, Officer and Knight (Chevalier).

The Royal Order of Sahametrei

The Royal Order of Sahametrei, established on 9 September 1948 by His Majesty King Norodom Sihanouk, is awarded as a token of the special friendship between Cambodia and foreign countries on individuals. The Royal Order of Sahametrei is given to foreigners who have rendered exceptional services to Cambodia, the Cambodian people, or the King of Cambodia. It is awarded in five classes: Grand Cross, Grand Officer, Commander, Officer and Knight.

The Royal Order of Queen Kossomak Nearireath

The Royal Order of Queen Kossomak Nearireath was established on 1 October 1962 by His Majesty King Norodom Suramarit and is awarded for distinguished services to the Throne in the following classes: Grand Cross, Grand Officer, Commander, Officer and Knight.

The Royal Order of Sowathara

The Royal Order of Sowathara was established on 22 June 1923 by King Monivong and is awarded for accomplishment in the fields of agriculture and economics in the following classes: Commander, Officer and Knight.

The Royal Order of Monisaraphon

The Royal Order of Monisaraphon was established by King Sisowath, originally in a single class, on 8 April 1905. It was raised to three classes on 9 September 1948 and to five in 1961. It is awarded for distinguished services in the fields of Education, Justice, Administration, Science, Literature and Fine Arts in the following classes: Grand Cross, Grand Officer, Commander, Officer and Knight.

GLOSSARY

Apsara A celestial water nymph, wife of the celestial musician known as "Gandharvas".

Ascetic A sage who practises austerities.

Ayutthaya The capital of Koshala which was ruled by Rama's father.

Brahma One of the three main Hindu gods, usually despicted with four arms and sometimes mounted on a vehicle known as a Hong.

Brahmin A Hindu priest.

Bossobok An open carved and gilded throne with a tapering roof and spire.

Deva A god or goddess. The word sometimes means a celestial creature inhabiting the lower levels of the Buddhist heaven.

Devi A title given to Parvati, wife of Shiva.

Garuda A mythological figure, half-man, half-bird. Widely used in architecture, particularly in royal buildings in Southeast Asia.

Hanuman Name of the white monkey general with magic powers, a leading character in the Ramayana epic.

Indra The Vedic God of the sky, clouds and monsoon and Guardian of the East.

Kinnari A mythical figure with the head and chest of a female and the body of a bird.

Krishna One of the incarnations of Vishnu.

Mondop A building in Khmer and Siamese style crowned with a seven-tiered spire.

Mount Kailasa Sacred mountain, residence of Shiva.

Mount Meru The mountain residence of the gods.

Naga A water serpent with many mythological associations—fertility, rainbows and creation. Widely used in architecture in Southeast Asia.

Ream Ker The Cambodian version of the Ramayana epic.

Shiva God of ascetics, and of cosmic destruction and creation.

Stupa A round Buddhist monument often domed, usually containing the ashes of a deceased personality or a sacred relic.

Nirvana The state of perfect bliss attained when the soul is freed from all suffering and absorbed into the supreme spirit.

BIBLIOGRAPHY

Aymonier, M. *Le Cambodge.* Paris. 1900. Vol. 1.

Chandler, David. *A History of Cambodia.* Silkworm Books. Chiangmai (Thailand). 1996.

Chou Ta-Kuan: The Customs of Cambodia, translated from the French edition by P. Pelliout. Siam Society. Bangkok. 1987.

Charles, L. *Un Voyage à la Cour du Roi Norodom.* S.G.C. de Bordeaux. Bordeaux. 1881.

Dumarcay, Jacques. *The Palaces of South East Asia,* edited and translated by M. Smithies. Oxford University Press. 1991.

Giteau, Madeleine. *History of Angkor.* Kailash Editions. Paris. 1997.

Groslier, Georges. *Recherches sur les Cambodgiens.* Paris. 1921.

Fuchs, Paul. *Fêtes et Cérémonies Royales au Cambodge d'Hier.* L'Harmattan. Paris. 1991.

Imbert, Jean. *Histoire des Institutions Khmeres.* Phnom Penh. 1961.

Henri, Lucien. *Promenade au Cambodge et au Laos, suivi d'une excursion à Bienhoa.* Ollendorf. Paris. 1894.

Loti, Pierre. *A Pilgrimage to Angkor,* translated from French by W.P. Baines and M. Smithies. Silkworm Books. 1996.

Moura, Jean. *Le Royaume du Cambodge.* Paris. 1883.

Phoeun, Mak. *Histoire du Cambodge.* EFEO. Paris. 1995.

Silvestre, A. *Le Cambodge Administratif.* Paris. 1924.

Sok, Khin. *Le Cambodge entre le Siam et le Vietnam, (1775-1860).* EFEO. Paris. 1991.

Vincent, Frank. *The Land of the White Elephant.* White Lotus. Bangkok. 1988. (Previously published by Sampson Low, Marston, Low and Searle of London in 1873.)

Rapport de la Mission Polono-Cambodgienne de Conservation des Monuments à Phnom Penh. 1985-1992.

The Grand Palace of Bangkok. The Office of His Majesty's Principal Private Secretary.1988.

Also documents and photographs from:
The Personal Archives of H. M. King Norodom Sihanouk
The Personal Archives of H.E. Madame Paulette Huot Sambath
The Personal Photo-Archives of Anna Price
The Personal Archives of Madame Madeleine Giteau
The Personal Archives of H.E. Ambassador Eng Roland
The Personal Archives of H.E. Thiounn Mumm
The Personal Archives of H.E. Ambassador Gerd Berendonck

Bibliothèque Nationale de Paris
Centre des Archives d'Outre-Mer, Aix-en-Provence, France
Library of Missions Étrangères de Paris
Musée Départemental Albert Kahn, Boulogne, France
National Archives of Cambodia, Phnom Penh
National Library of Cambodia, Phnom Penh
Revues Le Sangkum and Kambuja

We gratefully acknowledge the valuable support of the following sponsors:

Embassy of the Federal Republic of Germany (Phnom Penh)

Royal Netherlands Embassy (Bangkok)

AIR FRANCE

A RAFFLES International Hotel

The SHELL Company of Cambodia

The Ministry of Tourism of Cambodia   Bangkok Airways

H.E. Ambassador Truong Mealy • H.E. Pou Sothirak • H.E. Ambassador Fernando Gelbard